Broadband Economies

Creating the Community of the 21st Century

By Robert Bell,
John Jung and Louis Zacharilla

Published by the
Intelligent Community Forum

www.intelligentcommunity.org

First edition, published by Intelligent Community Forum, 55 Broad Street, 14th Floor, New York, NY 10004 USA – +1 646-291-6166, fax +1 212-825-0075 – www.intelligentcommunity.org

Acknowledgments

Many people and organizations have contributed to the evolution of the ideas presented in this book, and we are grateful for this chance to acknowledge them:

Janice Whyte, holder of many titles over a long career in the Chief Executive's office of the City of Sunderland, who introduced us to that extraordinary community and did so much to shape its future

Ma Ying-Jeou, President of Taiwan and former Mayor of Taipei, for his encouragement and support of ICF's vision and his personal leadership of Taiwan's evolution into an "Intelligent Nation"

Mayor Jeff Lukken, City Manager Tom Hall and Assistant City Manager Joe Maltese of LaGrange, Georgia, USA, who showed what a creative and determined rural community can do to build a broadband-based future.

Brenda Halloran, Mayor of the City of Waterloo, who led her city to become Intelligent Community of the Year and then adopted ICF's global mission as her own

Sylvie Albert and Rolland LeBrasseur of Laurentian University, and Don Flournoy of Ohio University, for contributing their time and considerable expertise to the development of ICF's analytic methods

Jerry Hultin, President of the Polytechnic Institute of New York University, and Mel Horwitch, Director of the Institute for Technology and Enterprise at NYU Polytechnic, who have hosted ICF's annual Summits and contributed their time and knowledge to the Forum's development

OneCommunity President Scot Rourke, who has set a global standard for social entrepreneurship in Intelligent Communities

The Board of Directors of the World Teleport Association, for incubating the Intelligent Community Forum as a special interest group of the association

The 79 (and counting) Intelligent Communities – and their hundreds of committed political, institutional and volunteer leaders – who have shared their stories with ICF while they continue to build the communities of the 21st Century

Contents

Communities in the 21st Century

It's all about the children.

Societies serve many purposes, but one outweighs all others. Societies exist to protect children. Like creatures whose first law is self-preservation, societies ensure their future by safeguarding the children who will bring it into being.

This is why, above all other crimes, we abhor the mistreatment of children: their neglect, their physical or mental abuse, their murder, their use as soldiers or drug dealers or prostitutes.

Communities are societies writ small. Whether small villages or immense cities, in developing nations or the industrialized world, their first priority is to be places where families can raise children, and where those children can build a future. That starts with access to the basics of human survival: clean water, food, shelter, safety. It also takes what *New York Times* columnist and author Thomas Friedman has called the "software of society" – the customs, laws and attitudes that give life meaning and the individual an understandable place in the culture. And it takes economic opportunity. Money may not buy you love, but economic opportunity makes possible everything else we value in a community. Without it, communities can stagnate and die in a few generations.

In 1900, the single largest source of employment in the United States was farming. By the end of the century, fewer than 3% of Americans were farmers. As a consequence, the vast middle portions of the country emptied out as children and their parents left rural homes and headed for, first, the cities, and then the suburbs and exurbs.

In the first decade of the 21st Century, the UN estimated that more than half of the world's people were living in cities for the first time in history. Much of the transformation has come from the rural poor in developing nations doing what Americans and Europeans did in earlier decades: fleeing to the cities in search of economic opportunity. They have done it in such numbers as to create a rising group of "mega-cities" with populations exceeding 10 million people. Of the 25 largest mega-cities, 19 are in developing nations.[1] And they are not through yet. The UN forecasts that, by 2030, three out of five people or 5 billion people will live in cities worldwide.

In the last quarter of the 20th Century, the same out-migration struck the manufacturing centers of the world's industrial nations. Decades of investment in automation raised productivity and reduced labor needs. At the same time, markets for most manufactured goods in the rich nations matured: consumers only need so many cars, refrigerators, washing machines and light bulbs in a lifetime. Adding to the impact – and making the most headlines – was "the rise of the rest:" a surge of economic growth and living standards in developing nations. Manufacturing moved to developing nations not only because they offered low-cost labor but because manufacturers expect them to be the next growth market for their products.

As a result, once proud manufacturing centers from Germany's Ruhr Valley to the American Midwest suffered the same fate as agricultural regions had in the past. A 1982 pop music hit, *Allentown,* by singer-songwriter Billy Joel captured the spirit of the times in America's "Rust Belt:"

> *Every child had a pretty good shot*
> *to get at least as far as their old man got.*
> *Something happened on the way to that place.*
> *They threw an American flag in our face.*

While the Rust Belt rusted, developing nations that escaped war and the extremes of bad governance started the long boom that continues today. Once mere assembly centers for components manufactured elsewhere, developing nations are striving with considerable success to become innovative producers of sophisticated equipment, systems and software. From 1990 to 2003, manufactured exports from developing nations rose 11.5% compared with 5.1% from industrialized nations. This was enough to boost developing nations' share of global exports from 20% to nearly 35%. China is the overwhelming leader: filter out China from the numbers, and the global share of manufactured exports from developing nations actually *fell* from 28.0% in 2000 to 27.4% in 2003. [2]

In the last decade of the 20th Century and first decade of the 21st, it began to seem that the industrialized world's once unshakeable grip on high technology employment would go the same way as agriculture and manufacturing. Offshoring began to move call center, data entry and then programming and systems jobs to developing nations. Headlines blared about X-rays being transmitted overseas to be read by Indian doctors, and US and European multinationals opening development centers in India, China, Vietnam and Malaysia.

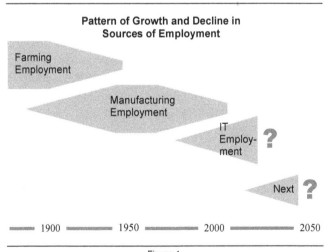

Pattern of Growth and Decline in Sources of Employment

Figure 1

It is easy to make too much of this. Manufacturing will not vanish from industrialized nations – in fact, manufacturing that demands high skills continues healthy job growth – and rising living standards in developing ones will gradually erode their cost advantage. A 2006 study from the Association for Computing Machinery noted that the job losses attributable to offshoring, estimated at 2-3% of the US IT workforce, were dwarfed by the normal cycle of IT job creation and loss in the American economy. [3]

Nevertheless, communities today are at an uncomfortable crossroads in both industrialized and developing nations. The sources of economic opportunity are changing faster than communities can naturally adapt. Manufacturing is following the pattern of farming, as illustrated in Figure 1, in which increasing productivity drastically erodes the number of people it employs. IT jobs are still on the growth track but will eventually follow the same pattern, only to be replaced by a new growth sector, such as biotechnology, sustainable energy or another candidate.

Communities must adapt continuously and at an ever greater rate or risk seeing cherished ways of life vanish while lack of opportunity bleeds them of the children who are their future. Succeeding in this new environment – which we call the Broadband Economy – takes conscious effort by government, business, institutions and individuals. It is not the product of the unfettered free market, nor of government policymakers alone, but of imaginative collaboration between the two. This book explains how to undertake it and describes what "Intelligent Communities" are already achieving.

The "how" and the "what" of creating an Intelligent Community make a long and complex story. But the "why?" That's simple.

It's all about the children.

What is an Intelligent Community?

The Broadband Economy

The Five Habits of Intelligent Communities

The Intelligent Community Indicators

CHAPTER 1

The Broadband Economy

In his bestselling book, *The World is Flat, New York Times* columnist Thomas Friedman reported on a conversation with Nanden Nilekani, CEO of India's Infosys. Mr. Nilekani had this to say on the topic of globalization:

> *"Outsourcing is just one dimension of a much more fundamental thing happening today in the world,"* Nilekani explained. *"What happened over the last [few] years is that there was a massive investment in technology, especially in the bubble era, when hundreds of millions of dollars were invested in putting broadband connectivity around the world, undersea cables, all those things"* At the same time, he added, computers became cheaper and dispersed all over the world, and there was an explosion of software – e-mail, search engines like Google, and proprietary software that can chop up any piece of work and send one part to Boston, one to Bangalore, and one part to Beijing, making it easy for anyone to do remote development. When all of these things suddenly came together around 2000, added Nilekani, they *"created a platform where intellectual work, intellectual capital, could be delivered from anywhere. It could be disaggregated, delivered, distributed, produced and put back together again – and this gave a whole new degree of freedom to the way we do work, especially work of an intellectual nature...And what you're seeing in Bangalore today is really the culmination of all these things coming together.* [4]

Beyond Globalization

At ICF, we don't feel that "globalization" does justice to the scope of this transformation, and to the way it is reshaping the economic lives of people around the planet. We call it the Broadband Economy – an economy in which for all intents and purposes the hard-working people of Bangalore and Beijing live right next door to the hard-working people of Boston, Brussels and Buenos Aires.

As Mr. Nilekani explained, the Broadband Economy is the product of the build-out of low-cost, high-speed communications and information technology on both the global and local levels. It began in the 1970s, when the carriers began linking the world's economic centers with fiber optic networks. These made possible collaboration and cooperation across time zones and cultures that opened markets, boosted productivity, created employment and improved living standards.

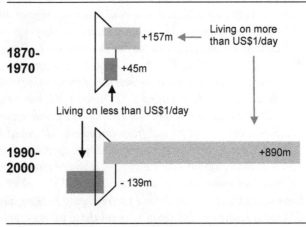

Figure 2

A simple set of numbers, illustrated in Figure 2, captures the power of this transformation. During the century from 1870 to 1970, the number of people living on more than US$1 per day, adjusted for inflation, grew by 157 million. At the same time, however, the number living on less than 1 dollar a day also grew by 45 million. Still, not bad: a net 112 million people moved out of abject poverty over a century. But compare that to the *ten years* from 1990 to 2000. The number of people living on more than 1 dollar a day grew by 890 million, while the number living on less *shrank* by 139 million. That's a net *one billion people* moving up in a single decade.

What made it happen? No single factor could account for such an enormous change. But in any comparison between the decade and the century, you would have to put the availability, from 1990 to 2000, of advanced digital communications at the top of a list.

Using the broadband infrastructure, companies began to look for opportunities to locate their facilities where they could gain the greatest advantage in terms of costs, skills and access to markets. The deployment of global broadband also made capital investment highly mobile. Billions of US dollars move around the globe daily in pursuit of a competitive return, and when trouble strikes a nation's economy, that mobile capital can also flee at devastating speed.

For communities, local economic success has come to depend on the global economy in ways never before imagined. But while global business may be mobile, communities are not. Communities everywhere have the same goal: to be a place where people can raise their children and give those young people enough economic opportunity to allow them to stay and raise children of their own. In the Broadband Economy, that task is more challenging than ever.

The Broadband Paradox

Geographic location and natural resources were once the key determiners of a community's economic potential. In one person's lifetime, they changed seldom if at all. But in the Broadband Economy, it is increasingly the skills of the labor force, and the ability of business and government to adapt and innovate, that power job creation. And these are assets that must be continually replenished.

Why has this change occurred? As economic centers are connected, it becomes possible to manage distant facilities as though they were across the street. That means, in the Broadband Economy, that every worker is exposed to wage and skill competition from every other worker in similar industries around the world. This has shifted demand for low-skilled labor – the kind used in extracting resources from the Earth and basic manufacturing – to low-cost countries in the developing world. When you visit those booming countries, however, the business press is full of worry about lack of skills and innovation. Even countries in the early stages of industrial growth are feeling the same competitive pressures that have become acute in industrialized nations.

Intelligent Communities are those which have come to understand the enormous challenges of the Broadband Economy, and have taken conscious steps to create an economy capable of prospering in it.

Employment insecurity has risen and will continue to increase worldwide as businesses face global competition and go global in search of talent. The only jobs that are immune to the pressures of the Broadband Economy – local retailing and services from plumbing to real estate – do not bring new money into a community; they merely move it around from pocket to pocket within the community. A sustainable community must have inputs and outputs, which means external markets for the skills, services and products it provides.

Intelligent Communities are those which have – whether through crisis or foresight – come to understand the challenges of the Broadband Economy, and have taken conscious steps to create an economy capable of prospering in it. They are not necessarily big cities or famous technology hubs. They are located in developing nations as well as industrialized ones, suburbs as well as cities, the hinterland as well as the coast.

The good news is that, while the Broadband Economy presents an epic challenge to communities, it also hands them a powerful new competitive tool. Beginning in the 1990s, carriers deployed the local networks that most of us think of as "broadband" – DSL, cable, satellite and wireless – within neighborhoods, towns and cities. At the same time, the costs of computer software and hardware – especially data storage – plummeted in obedience to Gordon Moore's famous law that the storage capacity of microchips doubles every 18 months. Through local broadband, individuals, small businesses, institutions and local governments have gained access to worldwide information resources and a broad range of tools to connect both globally and locally. In the 1970s, these were the exclusive province of multinational corporations and major institutions. Today, they are as close as the computer on your desk or the mobile device in your pocket.

Today, broadband offers every community the opportunity to move from the periphery to the center in economic terms. It creates new kinds of companies like Yahoo and Google, even whole new industries. It enables local companies to be global exporters – including the export of skills and knowledge which were never before transportable across time zones or national borders.

It can ensure that schools in remote regions and inner cities have access to the latest information tools and reference sources. It can link local healthcare providers to leading medical centers and local law enforcement to national information grids. Individuals and businesses can go global in search of low-cost, quality vendors, and Web-based tools can increase community involvement.

By boosting the economic and social well-being of communities, broadband can reduce the incentives for their young people to move away in search of opportunity and a better quality of life. Paradoxically, it can play a key role in giving communities a sustainable future in our ever-more-connected world.

Broadband in the Local Economy

- Creating new companies and new industries
- Empowering local companies to be global exporters
- Enabling export of skills and knowledge
- Providing schools with access to the latest information
- Linking local healthcare to leading medical centers
- Connecting local law enforcement to national data grids
- Allowing local businesses and individuals to go global in search of low-cost, high-quality vendors
- Strengthening community involvement with Web-based tools

But broadband is no magic bullet. Technology alone will not create a prosperous and inclusive economy, which is the foundation for everything else that makes a community healthy and vital. Intelligent Communities work long and hard, in many different ways, to adapt to the challenges of the Broadband Economy. Some are recovering from economic crisis and have more plans and hopes than tangible results to show. Others are well on the way toward ambitious goals and have a record of achievement to display. Some far-sighted communities never let crisis overtake them in the first place, but made the right choices and investments in time to benefit from the emergence of the Broadband Economy. This book is about their stories and the lessons they can teach us all.

CHAPTER 2

The Five Habits of Intelligent Communities

The "hardware" of society is easily understood. It is the infra-structure of transport and roadways, commercial buildings, residential housing, utilities, communications systems, and so on. It's easy to see and easy to value in dollars or euros or yen.

The "software" of society is less visible. It is the laws and how they are enforced. It is the subtle rules of the culture, but also the tolerance shown those who bend those rules. It is the identity of the people: whether they place greater value on the individual or the community. Whether they prefer freedom or order. Whether they believe in fair play or think the winner should take all.

Social software is powerful. To appreciate its power, you need look no further than the world's oil producing nations. In some of them, people enjoy very high standards of living. In others, the majority of people are so poor they have no running water, sanitation or medical care. You have probably heard the term used to describe these resource-rich countries where pov-erty reigns. It is "the oil curse." Instead of going to fund infra-structure or education, oil money flows into the pockets of the ruling elite. Corruption is rampant. Oil so dominates the economy that sectors from farming to manufacturing stagnate and wither.

What's the difference between a nation that lets its people share in oil wealth while investing it wisely for the future, and a nation that wastes it on a corrupt elite while millions suffer? It's the ability of the society's software to handle the rush of black gold.

Though you will never see drillers celebrating over a gusher of megabits, broadband is another source of potential prosperity. And for community leaders everywhere, it presents a similar question: will the Broadband Economy be a blessing or a curse? Some communities have shown themselves to be very effective in adapting to the demands of the Broadband Economy. They are the ones that show up on the Intelligent Community Forum's Smart21 and Top Seven lists each year. (See page 163 for more information.) But how do they get there? What are the common factors that make them success- ful? In the rest of this book, we will talk about specific issues – called Intelligent Community Indicators – where Intelligent Communities put their focus. But behind the strategies that can be studied and adapted, other factors are at work: the social software made up of culture and experience and habit. Before talking about Indicators or infrastructure, it is worth- while understanding the habits of communities that are highly effective n the Broadband Economy.

Intelligent Communities have five habits that separate them from the rest. Here's the first:

> **Intelligent Communities have leaders who convince their people that there is more to be gained than lost from plugging into the Broadband Economy.**

For most of us, this is not an intuitive thing. If we live in an industrialized nation, we read about or experience jobs moving to lower-wage countries. We feel new wage pressure and performance demands brought about by rising competition. We feel confusion and even fear in the face of foreign cultures that seem to be invading us and changing how we live. If you live in a developing nation, connecting to the global economy brings new opportunity but risks overturning age-old traditions that give meaning to life, and often brings young and old into conflict. In any community, the costs and benefits are not evenly distributed. There are clear losers among those lacking education, skills, energy and adaptability, and clear winners among the better educated and better connected.

Somehow, leaders of Intelligent Communities bridge these differences. They help the majority of citizens understand the threats and opportunities facing the community and how each can make a difference. They find ways to channel fear and doubt into hope and aspiration. And they do these things because, as human beings, they care less about achieving political victories than about achieving real ones. Leaders interested only in winning the next election need not apply.

Intelligent Communities are open to change.

If the majority of your citizens believe that life stops at the municipal borders – that only local issues, events and people are important – you are in trouble. Because there is a globe full of people in competition with you who think your borders don't matter. If you want to see the impact of being closed rather than open, take a look at the US automotive industry. Toyota made headlines in 2007 when its quarterly sales outpaced General Motors for the first time. How did they do it? For most of its history, Toyota has targeted global markets, learned what consumers in those markets wanted, and then focused relentlessly on delivering a high quality product at low cost. The same could not always be said about America's Big Three car companies. During the administration of US President Ronald Reagan, the CEOs of the Big Three went to Japan with the US Secretary of Commerce to "force open" the Japanese market. In all of the reporting, one detail jumped out. The Japanese drive on the left-hand side of the road, as do the British, Australians and Indians. At that time, all of the cars the Big Three were trying to sell in Japan were equipped only to drive on the right-hand side of the road – where Americans drive – and they just couldn't understand why those protection-ist Japanese weren't buying them.

If you visit Issy-les-Moulineaux[a] in France, you will find a community that knows how to be open rather than closed. Mayor Andre Santini was first elected in 1980 and he set his sights on making technology the backbone of the local economy. One story illustrates how openness to the world made a difference. In 1994, Mayor Santini asked city depart-ments to study the development of the Internet in the US, and to incorporate what they learned in their plans for the future.

Stop for a moment and think. In 1994, the Web was still not much more than a curiosity. It was in 1994 that Netscape introduced the first widely used Web browser. There were only 10,000 Web sites in the world, compared with over 80 million in 2006. Yet an open community like Issy was alert to change and prepared to learn from anyone, anywhere.

If Issy-les-Moulineaux was open to the world, Dundee, Scotland,[b] was open to what was going on in its own back yard. From the mid 1970s to the mid 1990s, global economic changes swept over this industrial city and left it a hollowed-out shell in apparently terminal decline. City government worked hard to reverse the trend but nothing seemed to help. But the city also devoted scarce resources to measuring what was going on in the economy, in the same way that intensive care units monitor their patients' vital signs.

In the late 1990s, the squiggly lines on the monitor unex-pectedly made an upward jog. For the first time in a genera-tion, the city experienced net job growth, even as it continued to lose manufacturing jobs. More research followed, and the city discovered that its university sector had emerged as a driver of economic growth. Not that the schools themselves were doing the hiring. Instead, they were seeding new clusters

---

[a] 2007 Top Seven Intelligent Community
[b] 2007-08 Top Seven Intelligent Community

of young companies in fields like computer games, software, animation, film, television and life sciences.

Open for Business in Dundee

- Relentlessly measured employment and job creation, and detected the first net job growth in late 1990s
- University sector had emerged as driver of economic growth, stimulating new clusters of knowledge-driven, broadband-dependent start-ups in computer games, software, animation, film, TV and life sciences
- Government, universities and business collaborated to nurture growth

---

Today, the once dominant manufacturing sector provides only 10% of Dundee's jobs, while digital media employs over 2,300 people, life sciences another 4,000 and one of the world's biggest pharmaceutical companies has decided to base a major medical research center there.

> **Intelligent Communities develop inspiring visions and set ambitious goals.**

Intelligent Communities see visions – really big visions. They set ambitious goals, knowing full well that the goals may be beyond reach. In 1991, Tallinn[a] was the capital of a newly independent Estonia. After five decades of Soviet rule, its economy, infrastructure and government were in shambles. In 1995, the government set a goal – calling it a "Tiger Leap" – to provide every school with a PC and Internet connection by 1999. This was at a time when school buildings were falling apart and teachers earned the equivalent of 100 US dollars a month. What a crazy thing to do. Yet the Tiger Leap lit the fuse of an economic rocket. Today, every school and public

---

[a] 2007-2008 Top Seven Intelligent Community

building is online, but that's old news. After 10 years of GDP growth of more than 5% a year, per-capita income is still only about 40% of the average of the European Union's 15 original members – but a wireless network covers 90% of the country and Internet use is well above the European average.

You would think that, in Ottawa-Gatineau,[a] they don't need big visions. Ottawa is Canada's capital, after all, and it can safely count on having the world beat a pathway to its door. (Gatineau is its sister city in the French-speaking province of Quebec.) But the vision of this community is to be known, not as a political capital, but as the "Innovation Capital." More than 1,800 high-tech firms already employ 11% of the labor force, but local government is doing everything imaginable to increase that percentage: training and supporting entrepreneurs, attracting venture capital, and investing in workforce development.

Sunderland,[b] an English community near the Scottish border, had an unemployment rate of 22% in the 1980s as its heavy industrial economy collapsed. In 1994, the city fell into the bottom 10% of Britain's "depressed districts." The legacy of heavy industry was a large unemployed group of low-skilled workers, many with chronic health problems. With so little local opportunity, young people fled, leaving behind a shrinking and aging population.

So local government decided to build a completely new economy based on something called "telematics," which is a European term for the union of communications and computers. Sure. What could be more obvious? We have a community full of out-of-work shipbuilders and coal-miners, and we're going into telematics.

Well, they did. By 2006, Sunderland was the site of several award-winning technology parks, had created tens of

---

[a] 2007 Top Seven Intelligent Community
[b] 2003-07 Top Seven Intelligent Community; 2007 Lifetime Achievement Award Winner

thousands of new jobs and boosted its job creation rate above the British average. EDS opened its first data center in the north of England in Sunderland, one of many such decisions that allowed Sunderland to capture 72% of the new jobs in the region from 2002 to 2004, despite having just 11% of the north's population. Unrelenting activism about deploying broadband, and willingness to create joint ventures where necessary, convinced carriers to provide broadband at competitive costs at speeds up to 10 Mbps. Broadband penetration leaped from 25% in 2004 to 75% in 2006. The City Council has taken advantage of this connectivity to create an e-government portal that delivers a wide range of services to about 30,000 visitors per month. Broadband is also the medium for a Virtual Learning Environment created by the City of Sunderland College that is used by more than 20,000 students for training in information technology.

Dreaming Big, Achieving Big in Sunderland

- Faced post-industrial legacy: 1980s unemployment rate of 22%, 1994 rating in bottom 10% of UK "distressed districts," population with low educational achievement and chronic health problems
- Became, by 2006, home to award-winning tech parks, including first EDS data center in North of England
- Captured 72% of new jobs in the region from 2000 to 2004, despite having just 11% of the population
- Achieved 76% broadband penetration at up to 10 Mbps

Sunderland's success had nothing to do with luck, which was in short supply in the 1980s and 1990s. Rather, it was the product of hard and skillful work. Like Tallinn, they could have failed anywhere along the road, but by setting their sights high, they gained something to fight for.

Intelligent Communities create heroes.

"Heroes" are highly visible winners and local champions who understand that their achievement is not just the result of their own talents and hard work but is rooted in the community.

Both Dundee and Sunderland began their work by forming much heralded Partnerships – groups of citizen leaders representing all of their important constituencies – to help identify problems and develop solutions. In Sunderland, they went on to create "Community e-Champions," volunteers who are trained to carry the message and methods of digital inclusion to neighbors who would otherwise be left out.

Waterloo[a] in Canada is one of several small cities making up Canada's Technology Triangle. With about 10% of the Triangle's labor force, it accounts for 45% of job growth. Its success has been based on successful university-business partnerships. In the 1970s, the University of Waterloo established a policy that allowed students and faculty members to own rights in intellectual property they developed at the University. When the introduction of the personal computer began a decades-long wave of ICT growth, Waterloo was positioned to benefit. Like Stanford University in Silicon Valley, it spurred spin-outs of technology-based businesses, and local entrepreneurs began to build companies at a great rate. Fast-forward a few decades and the Waterloo region is a place where investors have poured C$1.8 billion (US$1.5bn) over the past 10 years into acquiring privately-held technology companies.

What distinguishes Waterloo from other tech cities is the extent to which the community celebrates its entrepreneurial heroes and the degree to which those people give back to the community. In 2000, the city undertook a year-long project called Imagine!Waterloo. Prominent citizens led a city-wide public consultation to determine the best possible future for the city. Its recommendations ranged from environmental protec-

---

[a] 2007 Intelligent Community of the Year; 2006-07 Top Seven Intelligent Community

tion to transportation, culture to city communications. Every autumn, Waterloo celebrates Entrepreneur Week, North America's largest innovation festival. Waterloo business leaders like Jim Balsillie, Chairman of Research in Motion, are honored for serving on steering committees and funding local institutes. Mr. Balsillie and his peers have supported continuing innovation by founding the Center for International Governance Innovation (CIGI), the Perimeter Institute for Theoretical Physics, the Institute for Quantum Computing, the Waterloo Technology StartUp Network, and Communitech, a capacity-building association focusing on technology in the region.

Celebrating Heroes in Waterloo

- The Imagine!Waterloo public consultation project placed business and university leaders at the head of an effort to determine the city's best possible future
- The annual Entrepreneur Week is North America's largest innovation festival
- Waterloo honors entrepreneurs who reach into their pockets to fund local institutes and centers of excellence

---

Intelligent Communities do this work consciously and continuously, because it achieves so many goals. By creating heroes, they establish role models for the behavior they want to encourage. By involving those heroes in decision-making, they open up the process to new ideas. And by enlisting those heroes in the resulting programs, they gain ambassadors to "sell" the necessary changes to the community.

> **Intelligent Communities avoid falling in love with technology.**

Intelligent Communities don't expect a particular technology – like municipal WiFi or e-government – to be a magic cure for what ails them. When community leaders ask what kind of broadband technology they should acquire – wireless, fiber, hybrid – our answer is always the same: it is literally the last thing you should worry about. Worry about creating a workforce able to do knowledge work. Worry about boosting the level of innovation in your local economy. Worry about creating reasons for people to use broadband. Information and communications technology changes at light speed. Whatever you or your private-sector partner ultimately invests in, you can be sure it will change many times over the next decade.

E-Government in Gangnam

1990-1995	Developed local area network to deliver e-government services through public kiosks
1995-2000	Converted LAN-based e-government system into Web portal accessible by anyone with an Internet connection
2006	Launched TV GOV interactive digital broadcast system to bring e-government to non-computer users
2008	Began introduction of ubiquitous computing services integrating IT, mobile, wireless and GPS

No Intelligent Community understands this better than the Gangnam district[a] of Seoul, South Korea's capital. In 1995, only 1% of South Koreans used the Internet. Today, the nation is the world's leader in broadband Internet penetration. The civic leadership of Gangnam has invested heavily in technology over the past 20 years. The vision has been consistent, but the technology has undergone regular transformation. In the 1990s, Gangnam built a local area network and installed kiosks to give citizens access to over 60 e-government applica-

---

[a] 2008 Intelligent Community of the Year; 2006-08 Top Seven Intelligent Community

tions. By the end of the decade, they converted this traditional network system into a Web portal accessible by anyone with a browser. At the end of 2006, Gangnam launched TV GOV, an interactive digital broadcast system on the world's most widely accepted platform: television. The next step will be so-called "ubiquitous" services that integrate IT, mobile, wireless and GPS systems. And the next time Gangnam is in the headlines, it will probably be for pioneering the next big thing in information and communications technology.

That's the software of Intelligent Communities. They have leaders who convince their people, often despite themselves, that there is more to be gained than lost from embracing the Broadband Economy.

They are open to new evidence, innovative ideas and new solutions, and don't allow common wisdom to blind them to what is happening in the community and outside it.

They have big, ambitious visions of where they can go next, despite the many obstacles they face.

They consciously and consistently create local heroes, who understand that their success is rooted in the community and who want to give something back.

And they resist the siren song of the latest hot technology, knowing that technology is always changing, and that it does not matter what they have so much as how they use it.

The bad news about habits is that they are hard to break. It's true in your personal life, and true in the life of your community. Much of the work that Intelligent Communities do comes down to breaking old habits embedded in the mind and the culture and replacing them with new ones.

The fact that habits are hard to break, however, is also the good news. Once you do the hard work of replacing old habits with new ones, the new ones tend to stick. The vicious cycle becomes the virtuous one. What was considered to be the un-avoidable fate of the community becomes its exciting future. When it comes to creating sustainable change, the hardware of society plays a role, but it is the software that really counts.

CHAPTER 3

Introducing the Indicators

In 2001, the Province of Ontario asked the authors to conduct a horizontal study of six "smart cities" in North America and Europe. The purpose was to find a meaningful way to compare the cities' progress toward the elusive goal of becoming "intelligent."

The result was ICF's Intelligent Community Indicators: the first conceptual framework for understanding the factors that determine a community's competitiveness in the Broadband Economy. Since that time, ICF has worked to refine and clarify the five Indicators, and to develop quantitative measurements for each one, which have become the basis for our Intelligent Community Awards program. Here they are:

---

1. Broadband Connectivity

Broadband connectivity is Internet access at speeds higher than dial-up, provided by DSL, cable modem, wireless, high-capacity data line or satellite. Broadband speeds range from a low of a few hundred kilobits per second up to 100 Mbps and beyond. Broadband is the new essential utility, as vital to economic growth as clean water and good roads. Intelligent Communities express a clear vision of their broadband future and craft public policies to encourage deployment and adoption. Some communities are well served by private sector carriers, and focus their efforts on promoting digital inclusion and boosting adoption. Others deploy broadband to fill coverage gaps or provide service where no private company is willing to invest. Strategies include public policies that encourage broadband development, creating networks to serve government facilities, public-private partnerships that serve businesses and citizens, dark fiber and open-access networks and direct competition with the private sector.

2. Knowledge Workforce

A knowledge workforce is a labor force that creates economic value through the acquisition, processing and use of information. Broadband has made knowledge the major economic driver it is today, by allowing multinational companies to tie together their global operations and create global markets for products and services. And it is the rise of knowledge work that makes broadband the next essential utility for communities seeking sustainable prosperity. By its very nature, knowledge gains economic value by being transmitted and broadband has become the Silk Road of the 21st Century knowledge worker. Companies whose output is information have become the global darlings of the business world from Microsoft and Google to Bharti Airtel and Reuters.

Intelligent Communities demonstrate the determination and ability to develop a workforce qualified to perform knowledge work. This does not just mean cranking out graduate students in science and engineering. As information technology becomes part of ever more processes, knowledge work extends from the factory floor to the research lab, and from the loading dock to the call center or Web design studio.

3. Digital Inclusion

The Broadband Economy promises to usher in a golden age of prosperity, knowledge and freedom. But it has just as much potential to usher in a "gilded age," where the benefits go to a privileged few and fail to ignite economic growth. As broadband deploys widely through a community, there is serious risk that it will worse the exclusion of people who already play a peripheral role in the economy and society, whether due to poverty, lack of skills, prejudice or geography. Deeper exclusion increases income inequality and all of the ills that go with it, while raising yet another obstacle to social mobility and ultimately impoverishing the whole community. Intelligent Communities promote digital inclusion by creating policies and funding programs that provide "have-nots" with access to digital technology and broadband, by providing skills training and by promoting a compelling vision of the benefits that the Broadband Economy can bring to all citizens.

4. Innovation

For business, broadband has become to innovation what fertilizer is to farming. Broadband makes it cheaper and faster to acquire the knowledge on which all forms of innovation are based. It gives innovators access to talent from around the world and provides global market access even to small and midsize companies.

Intelligent Communities focus on creating, attracting and retaining knowledge workers, because it is one of the most important steps they can take to raise their innovation rate. They also work to build the local innovation capacity of new companies, because these produce all of the job growth in modern economies. Strategies include breaking through bureaucratic barriers to business formation, creating a talent pipeline for local businesses, and improving access to markets and risk capital that fast-growth businesses require. Intelligent Communities also invest in e-government programs that reduce their costs while delivering services on the anywhere-anytime basis that digitally savvy citizens expect.

5. Marketing and Advocacy

With markets, capital and business operations more global than ever before, employers and citizens enjoy the biggest range of location choices in history. Like businesses facing greater global competition, communities must work harder than ever to communicate their advantages and explain how they are maintaining or improving their position as wonderful places to live, work and build a growth business. That communication has two aspects: outbound *marketing* to sell the community to talented individuals, entrepreneurs and established organizations, and inbound *advocacy* to sell the community on itself.

The Intelligent Community Indicators provide communities with a framework for assessment, planning and development, as they work to build prosperous local economies in the Broadband Economy. The Indicators also reveal the interactions that can create a "virtuous cycle" of positive change.

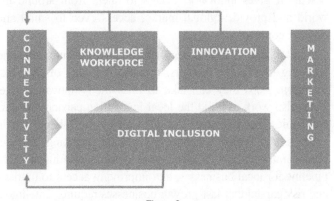

Figure 3

1. Broadband connectivity stimulates the development of a knowledge workforce. It provides the information and communications technology (ICT) tools that knowledge

workers need, as well as access to the entertainment, knowledge and services they demand.

2. Local connectivity creates a need for digital inclusion, to which Intelligent Communities respond with access and training. As people in the community employ ICTs in their life and work, it models behavior for the digitally excluded and encourages them to gain skills and use free and low-cost ICT provided by the community.

3. Growth in the population of knowledge workers employing ICT promotes innovation, as does the growth in new users created by digital inclusion programs.

4. Knowledge work, innovation and digital inclusion all drive growth in the demand for broadband and IT-based services in work, life and governing.

5. Connectivity, knowledge work, innovation and digital inclusion create a powerful story for marketing the community's strengths to outsiders as well as advocating for continued improvement within the community.

Success Factors

Since the original study, ICF has also identified factors that distinguish the most successful Intelligent Communities.

Collaboration. The development of an Intelligent Community typically requires intense collaboration among government, businesses, universities and institutions. Few organizations have enough resources, political capital or public backing to drive a community-wide transformation. But collaboration is challenging. It demands vision, flexibility, and a high degree of trust among the partners. Intelligent Communities develop the vision, find the flexibility and create trusting relationships among key constituencies. Effective collaboration is typically the result of the working environment created by effective leaders.

Leadership. It is fair to say that no Intelligent Community has succeeded without strong leadership. Effective leaders identify challenges, set priorities, communicate a compelling vision and foster a sense of urgency in achieving it. They establish a collaborative environment that encourages risk-taking and creates win-win relationships with partners in government, businesses and institutions. In the Intelligent Communities that ICF has studied, leadership has emerged from elected officials, government employees, business executives, universities and nonprofit organizations. What matters are the character, motivation and talents of the individuals who commit themselves to improving the economic and social well-being of the community.

Sustainability. When Intelligent Communities invest in broadband, workforce development, digital inclusion, innovation and marketing, they work to create programs that sustain themselves through local service revenue, growth of the tax base, and the attraction of long-term investment. They avoid depending on short-term funding that fails to lay a foundation for the future, or that is subject to changing political priorities. They also plan their growth in order to maintain quality of life while creating jobs and spurring business growth. They craft policies on land use, building codes, transportation, rights-of-way and other infrastructure to ensure the community remains a desirable place to live and work. They also use technology to reduce dependence on physical infrastructure, allowing more citizens to share the same community resources. And many Intelligent Communities give specific attention to environmental sustainability. They invest in Intelligent Community programs in order to identify environmental issues, reduce pollution and curb carbon emissions as well as for economic development and inclusion.

How to Become an Intelligent Community

Broadband Connectivity

Knowledge Workforce

Digital Inclusion

Innovation

Marketing and Advocacy

CHAPTER 4

Broadband Connectivity

The development of telecommunications has followed different paths in different places, but the stories have much in common. At their heart is tension between telecommunications as a business and telecommunications as a public good – between the profit motive and a public-service mandate.

Typically, development begins as a business venture. Investors become convinced of the potential of a new system, and businesses develop and deploy it. As the business model proves itself, more investment rushes in, focused on the most profitable markets and often sacrificing quality of service in a rush to gain market share. At some point, often as providers teeter on the edge of bankruptcy, government steps in, either to make rules governing access and quality for what has become a broadly-used public service, or to acquire the assets and run the telecommunications infrastructure itself.

In much of the world, national governments became the telecommunications operators through state-owned companies such as France Telecom, Nippon Telegraph & Telephone, Embratel and Telekom South Africa. In the US, development took a different course, largely through the efforts of Theodore Vail, the first president of AT&T, who convinced state regulators that the public would benefit more from having a privately-held monopoly provider buy up floundering local telephone companies and guarantee a high level of service at an affordable price.

Since the 1980s, there has been an overwhelming global move in the opposite direction: to eliminate monopolies and sell off state-owned telephone companies. Early competitive providers like MCI in the US pointed the way by demonstrating that competition could drastically lower long-distance telephone costs and provide a more innovative range of services. When governed by transparent and impartial regulations to protect the public interest, competition appears to deliver the best value to customers and the best growth environment for the industry as a whole – if not for incumbents that formerly benefited from a stranglehold on the market.

The Broadband Race

Communications carriers around the globe have moved to deploy broadband – via xDSL, cable modem and wireless – to consumers, small businesses and institutions in the most profitable markets. The rate of deployment has varied drastically from nation to nation. The Organization for Economic Cooperation and Development, a membership organization for the world's industrial economies, provides a portal reporting on broadband penetration, services and speeds. Its June 2007 report showed the following breakdown of broadband penetration per 100 people in the 30 OECD member countries:

OECD Broadband statistics

OECD Broadband subscribers per 100 inhabitants, June 2007

Rank		DSL	Cable	Fiber	Other	Total
1	Denmark	21.3	9.7	2.9	0.4	34.3
2	Netherlands	20.4	12.7	0.4	0.0	33.5
3	Switzerland	20.5	9.3	0.0	0.9	30.7
4	Korea	10.1	10.6	9.2	0.0	29.9
5	Norway	22.7	4.5	1.8	0.7	29.8
6	Iceland	29.0	0.0	0.2	0.6	29.8
7	Finland	24.4	3.7	0.0	0.8	28.8
8	Sweden	17.9	5.6	4.6	0.4	28.6
9	Canada	11.9	12.9	0.0	0.1	25.0
10	Belgium	14.5	9.2	0.0	0.1	23.8
11	UK	18.4	5.3	0.0	0.0	23.7
12	Australia	18.3	3.4	0.0	0.9	22.7
13	France	21.4	1.1	0.0	0.0	22.5
14	Luxembourg	19.8	2.4	0.0	0.0	22.2
15	United States	9.3	11.5	0.6	0.7	22.1
16	Japan	10.8	2.9	7.6	0.0	21.3

Rank		DSL	Cable	Fiber	Other	Total
17	Germany	20.2	1.0	0.0	0.1	21.2
18	Austria	11.4	6.6	0.0	0.6	18.6
19	Spain	13.3	3.6	0.0	0.1	17.0
20	New Zealand	14.6	1.1	0.0	0.8	16.5
21	Italy	15.4	0.0	0.4	0.0	15.8
22	Ireland	11.1	1.6	0.0	2.6	15.4
23	Portugal	9.2	5.4	0.0	0.1	14.7
24	Czech Rep.	5.5	2.5	0.3	3.9	12.2
25	Hungary	6.8	4.7	0.0	0.1	11.6
26	Poland	5.5	2.4	0.0	0.1	8.0
27	Greece	7.1	0.0	0.0	0.0	7.1
28	Slovak Rep.	3.9	0.8	1.1	1.0	6.8
29	Turkey	5.1	0.0	0.0	0.0	5.2
30	Mexico	3.5	1.0	0.0	0.1	4.6
	OECD	**11.6**	**5.4**	**1.4**	**0.3**	**18.8**

Figure 4

The annual publication of this list causes much hand-wringing in the nations, from the US to Germany, that appear lower on the list than they would like. Recent work from The Phoenix Center for Advanced Legal & Economic Public Policy Studies (www.phoenix-center.org) suggests, however, that as much of 90% of the variance is caused by factors including geography, educational achievement, social attitudes and culture that are beyond the reach of simple policy fixes. And despite concern over the "slow" pace of deployment, broadband has been one of the fastest-growing technologies in telecommunications history. According to a 2004 report by the UK-based research group PointTopic, it took mobile phones 5.5 years to grow from 10 million to 100 million subscribers worldwide. Broadband did it in 3.5 years.[5]

Nonetheless, as the economic potential of information and communications technology has become clear, broadband deployment has become an important local and regional issue. Local, state and provincial governments strive to ensure that their citizens and businesses have what it takes to succeed in an increasingly competitive global economy. The result is a revival of tensions between public and private sectors about building networks and deploying services.

Next-Gen Communications

Much of this book is devoted to broadband: its use, its challenges and its transformative impact on communities. But there is actually nothing important about broadband in and of itself. What *is* important is that, in industrialized nations, broadband represents the next generation in communications.

Before the Internet, one-to-one communications for most of us meant voice, either fixed line or mobile, with data and video transmission reserved for organizations that could afford its high cost. The arrival of the Web made both browsing Web sites and email – the killer app of the Internet – accessible to anyone who could afford a personal computer and a dial-up Internet connection. With broadband, the merger of computers and communications goes one step further. A broadband-enabled computer has access to virtually unlimited digital resources: information in text, graphic, audio and video formats, downloadable software, hosted services, real-time communications through instant messaging – the list goes on and on. In the days when dial-up was most people's only access to the Internet, there was a clear dividing line between software and files that resided on your own PC and those out on the Web. Minutes elapsed from the time of a mouse-click requesting something to its delivery. With a broadband connection, however, the distinction between your own PC and the Web blurs. The relatively cheap computer on your desk or lap reaches seamlessly in seconds around the globe.

In industrialized nations, there is a rising tide of argument in favor of fiber-to-the-home deployment providing speeds of 20-100 Mbps to residential users. Proponents believe that xDSL and cable broadband, which are still being deployed, will turn out to be a dead end because they will not support the emerging era of Web 2.0, video and rich-media applications.

Rather than allowing another bottleneck to form, the argument goes, it is better to deploy the essentially unlimited capacity of fiber now.

But the transformative impact of communications is not just about broadband. In 2007 in the United Kingdom, there were 66 Internet users per 100 people and 25 of them were on broadband. In Kenya, there were only 8 Internet users per 100 and only half of one percent was on broadband. But there

Internet/Mobile User Per 100

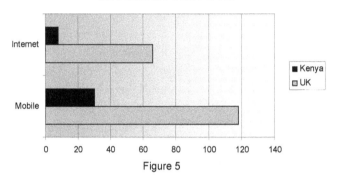

Figure 5

were 30 Kenyan telephone subscribers per 100 people that year, compared with 118 in the UK.   Put another way, a Brit in 2007 may have been 500 times more likely to be on broadband than a Kenyan, but only 4 times more likely to have a mobile phone. [6]

Access to mobile telephony has skyrocketed in Africa, from 37 million subscribers in 2002 to 270 million in 2007, a 48% compound annual growth rate. Nearly 90% of all phone lines in Kenya were mobile in 2007, compared with 68% in the UK and only 57% in the USA.[7] And it has had the same transformative impact for people who did not previously have a telephone as access to broadband has had in richer nations. The largest mobile carrier in Kenya, Safaricom, has seen its subscriber base rise from 20,000 in 2000 to over 10 million in 2008.   One of its most enduring achievements may be M-PESA, a pioneering service that enables Safaricom's customers to send money to each other by text message faster and cheaper than by conventional funds transfer. In 2008, it was moving US$1.5 million per day across Kenya, and the company had begun rolling the service out in India, Tanzania, Afghanistan and other markets.[8] The ability to send money by phone has multiple impacts. Day laborers can be paid by phone, as can taxi drivers, who thereby avoid carrying lots of cash around. Money can be sent to friends and family in emergencies. One popular practice is to deposit money before making a long journey and then withdraw it at the other end, which is safer than carrying lots of cash. For Safaricom's customers, M-PESA effectively lowers the barriers to trade, which has been as beneficial at the local level as it is on the international level. [9]

An August 2007 paper by Robert Jensen reported on what economists call a "natural experiment" that took place in Kerala, India between 1997 and 2006. The fishermen of Kerala, a region in the south of India, faced the usual problems of their trade in developing nations. With no information on prices being paid at different markets, they typically took their fish to the same local market. If that market was oversupplied, they might earn nothing for their catch. But traveling hours to another market with a highly perishable cargo was out of the question. In his study, Dr. Jensen was able to show that, on average, 5-8% of the total catch was wasted, and there were wide variations in the price of fish at the 15 beach markets he studied along the coast. But in 1997, mobile phones came to Kerala and fishermen began to use them to check on local markets while they were still at sea. The coverage spread gradually, giving Dr. Jensen the chance to study the impact on the fishermen's behavior, the price of fish and the amount of waste. What he found was that, as soon as coverage became available in a region, the percentage of fishermen who ventured beyond their local market rose from zero to 35%. At that point, no fish were wasted and the variation in price between markets dropped dramatically. This more efficient market benefited everyone. Fishermen's profits rose 8% on average and consumer prices fell by 4% on average. Higher profits meant the phones typically paid for themselves within two months. And the benefits seemed to endure over time. [10]

Mobile Phones Transform African Fishing

Before fishermen had access to mobile:

* 0% of fishermen sold outside their "home" market
* 5-8% of the total catch went to waste

After fishermen gained access to mobile:

* 35% of fishermen sold outside their "home" market
* 0% of total catch went to waste
* Consumer prices fell 4%
* Fishermen's profits rose 8%

In a separate study in 2005, Leonard Waverman of the London Business School found that an extra 10 mobile phones per 100 people (10% growth) in a typical developing nation leads to an additional 0.59 percentage points of growth in GDP per person. [11]

Though we will go on talking about broadband in the rest of this chapter, keep one thing in mind. The ways in which communities obtain broadband, promote its use and create digital cultures of use apply to any kind of next-gen communications. The tactics of implementation will vary depending on the technology, the level of development of the local economy and the culture of its people. But the basic strategies apply as well in the developing world as the industrial nations.

Why Government Gets Involved

Why do local, state or provincial governments get involved in bringing connectivity to their communities? There appear to be three reasons:

1. **The Connectivity Gap.** Broadband becomes a political and governance issue in communities that believe they suffer from a lack of affordable, high-quality access. The broadband gap may take several forms:

    - "Market failure," in which private-sector providers have not deployed broadband to a majority of the population (or at all)

    - Pricing that makes broadband unaffordable to some or most citizens

    - Quality of service that is judged inadequate, whether due to slow speeds, service interruptions or other factors

    Of the three areas of concern, market failure is generally the easiest to demonstrate objectively. If private-sector carriers have not deployed broadband at all, or deployed only down Main Street, there is clearly a lack of appetite to invest. Pricing and quality of service are more reflective of the expectations of the community.

2. **Connectivity "Holes."** Even in communities with ample broadband resources, there are often locations that go unwired. They may be old industrial zones, low-income neighborhoods, or areas that pose a geographic challenge to network developers.

3. **Connectivity Promotion.** Sometimes communities want to invest in broadband in order to make a statement. They may choose to wire (or "unwire") the local airport, central business district, parks or other zones as a marketing or business development effort. They are sending a message that their community "gets it" when it comes to the Broadband Economy.

The reasons are listed in order of decreasing political sensitivity. Connectivity promotion projects are by far the most common, because they are relatively easy. They involve a restricted area, frequently use government-owned assets such as light poles for deployment, and have a low and predictable cost. For these reasons, they involve little competition with the private sector. Identifying and filling connectivity holes brings the government into direct competition with private carriers, albeit in niche geographic markets in which the carriers have demonstrated little interest. And in seeking to address an overall connectivity gap, government sets up as a decision-maker concerning issues left to the market in most industrialized economies: where and when to invest, what price to charge, and what quality of service to provide for that price.

Local and regional governments have found many ways to involve themselves in spurring access to broadband for their constituents. The most successful have all begun with the same first step: establishing a clear vision and communicating why broadband access matters. Though broadband has been a wildly successful commercial service, it is still not as common or well understood as traditional infrastructure. If constituents believe that broadband is just about online music or games, they will not provide political support when it is needed. And if communities choose to invest public funds, they need detailed plans with well-defined goals and milestones.

Once communities know what they want to do and why, they typically follow one of five different strategies. The following are the strategies, with examples from the communities that have followed them.

1. Development Policy

Remaining safely within the bounds of traditional policy-making, governments direct the usual tools of development policy at broadband deployment. They offer tax credits and, craft rights-of-way policies to support network development (including laying conduit whenever they excavate streets. They conduct inventories of existing broadband networks and access points, and launch feasibility studies into building government-owned networks – at least partly in order to convince the private-sector that they mean business.

In **Loma Linda, California, USA**[a], city government created a Connected Community project that envisioned every building connected with a 10 Gbps network. As part of implementation, it created what it called The Loma Linda Standard for all new residential and commercial construction as well as remodeling affecting more than 50% of a structure. The standard defined how internal cabling, the "wiring closet," the demarcation and external conduit networks were to be constructed to ensure that every resident or tenant of every building had the potential to access high-speed broadband services. The standard created a "bias toward broadband" among developers that proved transformative for the community. From 2004 to 2007, nearly a dozen projects went into development that incorporated the Loma Linda Standard.

Loma Linda, California, USA

- Loma Linda Standard made all new and +49% retrofit residential and business construction "broadband ready"

Whittlesea, Victoria, Australia

- WIRED Development project required developers of sub-divisions to install conduit and grant ownership to city
- City agreed to lease conduit at attractive rates to carriers for FTTP deployment

The city of **Whittlesea, Victoria, Australia**[b] also seized the opportunity created by property development to set standards for a broadband future. Through a project it called WIRED Development, it changed local planning rules to

---

[a] 2007 Smart21 Community
[b] 2007 Smart21 Community

require developers to install conduit as part of sub-division development and to turn ownership over to the city. Technical specifications for the conduit were included in the new rules. As part of the deal, the city agreed to lease the conduit at very attractive rates to carriers for the installation of a fiber-to-the-home network and delivery of "triple play" services. In 2005, the first developer to apply the rules issued a tender covering an 8,000-home development.

2. Networks for Government

Local and regional governments are big users of communications services, and they are generally as free as any business to build private networks for their own use. They construct a fiber, wireless or coaxial network linking all government offices, schools, libraries, hospitals and other public facilities in order to reduce communication costs and gain new capabilities. Fears of terrorism have spurred many national governments to make funds available to communities to improve "first responder" communications, and communities have been quick to capitalize on this opportunity. They deploy wireless networks, using the fiber/coax network as a backbone, to extend network applications to police, fire and emergency medical service vehicles as well. Having built out this sophisticated network, such communities often match the hardware investment with investments in e-government applications that further reduce costs while improving service to constituents.

What does this activity have to do with improving public access to broadband? By making these investments in networks and services, government becomes a vital anchor tenant for broadband and stimulates demand for broadband services. Public investment will frequently attract carriers interested in building and managing the network under a managed service contract – and it can be a short step from there to deploying services to constituents as well. Successful e-government programs increase overall broadband demand, further enhancing the opportunities for the private sector.

The city of **Corpus Christi, Texas, USA**[a] installed a WiFi network in 2004 to automate the reading of utility meters for its municipal-owned utilities, saving substantial money and improving the accuracy of billing data. Once the network had proved itself in a pilot project, however, the city enlisted all of its departments to study current business practices and identify possible improvements and cost/time savings that could be gained by moving to all-electronic processes. After identifying and prioritizing over 80 potential business process improvements, the city decided to install a network covering the entire municipality. County, state, federal and independent agencies were invited to share the network to communicate with assets in the coverage area. Local colleges were enlisted to partner with local businesses to upgrade their information technology systems and find ways to use the network for communication, Web access, dispatch, fleet location, inventory control and Internet marketing. The Corpus Christi school district issued wireless laptops to students in disadvantaged areas with virtual textbooks, Internet connectivity, parent-teacher communications, lessons plans and other educational resource access. The local bus company even installed Internet service on buses serving express routes to entice commuters.

Corpus Christi, Texas, USA

- 2004 WiFi network, deployed to automate utility meter reading, saved money and increased accuracy
- Business process improvement project identified 80 additional opportunities for savings and provided business case for network expansion and upgrade
- Applications expanded on network backbone: universities helping local businesses upgrade IT, wireless laptop program for students, WiFi on the move for bus system

---

[a] 2007 Smart21 Community

Kabul, Afghanistan

- Government Communications Network linked ministries, provincial capitals and legislative districts
- Played essential role in the nation's first democratic election
- Adapted to connect isolated mobile phone switches, creating first modern communications network

Kabul, Afghanistan[a] is the unlikely location of another such government network project. Using funds from development agencies and the US government, this war-torn capital of Afghanistan has built a telecom-based foundation for government. It developed an IP-based Government Communications Network linking 42 ministries and offices in Kabul via optical fiber and microwave, and extended this core network to 34 provincial capitals via satellite. A District Communications Network pushed connectivity further out to Afghanistan's 337 legislative districts. Both networks were essential to conducting Afghanistan's first democratic election. But they also became the foundation for a telecom revolution. Mobile phone service in Afghanistan was limited to disconnected "islands" where people could place local calls but not connect to the outside world. Once the network was in place, the contractor turned it into a backbone for connecting the mobile switches scattered around the country, introducing the first modern communications service much of the country had ever known. Not surprisingly, communications traffic soared as the long pent-up demand found an outlet.

3. Public-Private Partnerships

In other cases, government sets its sights on building a public-access network from the start but chooses not to build, own or operate it. This decision may be driven by regulation, such as

---

[a] 2007 Smart21 Community

national or state/provincial laws forbidding the public sector from providing telecommunications services. Politics may play a role: more than one local or state/provincial government has gotten into hot water by building networks that are drastically underutilized and stir taxpayer anger. Or it may be a matter of culture; for example, a principle that government must never compete with the private sector.

Public-private partnerships take many forms, limited only by imagination and the legal framework in which the municipality operates. In **LaGrange, Georgia, USA**[a], the city negotiated a deal in the 1990s that motivated a cable television company to develop a state-of-the-art broadband network. The city issued a municipal bond to fund network construction under an agreement in which the cable carrier agreed to lease back the network for its own use, with lease payments covering the debt service on the bond. In addition, the city retained a percentage of bandwidth for its own use, and went on to become a network and IT services provider to communities throughout the county.

In **Northeast Ohio**[b], the city of Cleveland, Case Western Reserve University, and major healthcare, arts and cultural organizations formed a nonprofit called OneCommunity. OneCommunity forged partnerships with the region's telephone and cable carriers, under which the carriers donated unused fiber-optic circuits to OneCommunity and OneCommunity contracted for last-mile fiber and VPN services from the carriers on behalf of its member organizations. To make the deal, OneCommunity had to overcome resistance to the creation of what carriers at first viewed as a new competitor. Eventually, all parties agreed that, by helping the public and nonprofit sectors become better users of IT and telecom services, OneCommunity saved them

---

[a] 2000 Intelligent Community of the Year
[b] 2008 Top Seven Intelligent Community

money while simultaneously boosting demand for broadband across the region.

LaGrange, Georgia, USA

- City issued municipal bond to fund fiber backbone
- Cable carrier leased back the network, with lease payments covering bond debt service
- City reserved bandwidth for its own use, went on to become network and service provider throughout county

Northeast Ohio, USA

- City and top institutions formed OneCommunity nonprofit
- Negotiated with carriers to transfer dark fiber assets to OneCommunity in exchange for last-mile contracts
- OneCommunity reduced member costs while boosting demand for broadband across region

Sunderland, England, UK

- Series of public-private joint ventures stimulated demand for broadband in business, government and residents
- Motivated carriers to deploy broadband at up to 10 Mbps

Ottawa, Ontario, Canada

- Volunteer-driven Ottawa Rural Communities Network project built awareness and aggregated rural demand
- City funded one-third of C$3 million network deployment

In the poor North-of-England community of **Sunderland**[a], carriers could make no business case for investing in broadband. Beginning in the 1990s, the government entered a series of small public-private partnerships with emerging carriers and technology companies. One built "Teleport House" at a successful local business park to ensure connectivity to the park's tenants. Another created the "Sunderland Hub," an ISP and e-government network for local businesses and community centers. None was an overwhelming success

---

[a] 2003-07 Top Seven Intelligent Community; 2007 Lifetime Achievement Award Winner

in itself. But by demonstrating demand and the government's determination to ensure access to services, it ultimately motivated the UK's leading carriers to deploy broadband at competitive rates at speeds up to 10 Mbps.

In **Ottawa**[a], the capital of Canada, local government spurred the formation of a volunteer group, the Ottawa Rural Communities Network (ORCnet) to build awareness about broadband and aggregate demand in rural areas. Through workshops, community meetings and work with the telecom sector, ORCnet helped service providers build a business case for extending broadband into low-density markets. Local government invested C$1 million in a C$3 million public-private partnership that built out a rural broadband network to close the urban-rural gap.

4. Dark Fiber and Open Access Networks

Yet another variation on deployment strategy leverages the municipality's control of its roads and rights of way to encourage the private sector to invest. In these communities, government stops issuing permits to carriers to lay cable or fiber and instead builds its own comprehensive network of conduits throughout the municipality and lays "dark fiber" throughout the network. It then leases access to the fiber to carriers.

By digging up the streets once and then closing them to further construction, local governments protects their citizens from the disruption of repeated road work. Competitive carriers – though not necessarily incumbents – react positively, because starting up service becomes as quick and easy as connecting equipment to both ends of the circuit. The municipalities price the leases to cover their construction and maintenance costs as well as providing a positive return on investment. In some cases, the municipalities go a step further

---

[a] 2007 Top Seven Intelligent Community

by creating an "open-access network" platform that permits carriers to provision services faster and more cost-effectively, which tends to encourage competition and service innovation.

In Sweden, the city of **Karlskrona**[a], decided to make a revolutionary change in the way telecommunications services were provided within its borders. Based on its success in attracting the corporate headquarters for several mobile phone companies in the 1990s, Karlskrona branded itself "Telecom City" and directed its municipal utility company, to build and operate a fiber network serving business and government. The company, called Affarskverken, became a commercial ISP as well as a network operator. But the company's services failed to generate subscriber growth. In 2004, city leadership changed the rules, directing that Affarskverken exit the services business and become an open network platform on which other service providers would deliver services to customers. These service providers were strongly encouraged not to lock customers in with long-term contracts as the city sought to position itself as a test-bed for new services. The Affarskverken network was reconfigured to become a competition-neutral, open-access network that allowed service providers to build and manage services on demand. Over the next two years, new service providers flocked to the network, including seven ISPs, five IPTV providers, two VOIP companies as well as suppliers of movies, music and local news. A public-private partnership has also successfully deployed an IPTV telemedicine service to residents.

Karlskrona, Sweden

- Government-funded fiber carrier deployed fiber network to serve business and government customers
- After failing to gain subscribers, carrier converted to open access network on which other providers could deploy services while carrier operated "physical layer"
- Attracted IPS, IPTV, VOIP and video-on-demand suppliers

---

[a] 2007 Smart21 Community

Loma Linda, California, USA

- In support of Loma Linda Standard, built an open-access "transport only" fiber network
- Gave a wide range of service providers cost-competitive access to customers

Neunen, Eindhoven, Netherlands

- OnsNet ("Our Net") cooperative, with financial support from Dutch government, deployed FTTP network
- Financed operation and debt service from member fees
- Achieved 97% penetration in six months based on Broadband Social Covenant

Open-access networks are not confined to Europe. Not content with just setting development policy (see page 21), the California city of **Loma Linda** went on to invest nearly US$30 million to build an open-access fiber network to meet its own communications needs and interconnect the fast-expanding array of new developments and renovation projects. Like Karlskrona, Loma Linda entered the "transport" business without becoming a service provider: in the jargon of the telecom industry, it became a "carrier's carrier" rather than a competitor. The municipality owns and operates a city-wide IP matrix consisting of multiple, redundant fiber optic loops with wireless coverage areas serving residential and business customers. Building cabling systems and other networks can connect to the city network so long as they follow The Loma Linda Standard codes. There is no requirement that anyone connect to the Loma Linda network but as a public utility it is able to offer considerable cost savings over alternatives.

The OnsNet project in Neunen, part of the **Eindhoven**[a] metropolitan area in the Netherlands, has taken a unique "coop" approach to fiber deployment. OnsNet, which means "Our Net" in Dutch, is owned by its members, 7,500

---

[a] 2008 Smart21 Community

households in Neunen, including retirement and assisted living facilities for its large elderly population. OnsNet used a subsidy from the national government to generate the capital needed to deploy a fiber-to-the-home network but operates it from membership fees.

The supposedly high cost of fiber deployment, says Kees Rover, is high only for a carrier seeking to run fiber to thousands of homes. For the individual homeowner, it is a relatively small cost for a home improvement that will boost the value of the property.

The coop was created by Kees Rover, CEO of a nonprofit management company called Close the Gap, and Henri Smits, director of the local housing association. Within six months of lighting the network, OnsNet had a 97% penetration rate, essentially eliminating the market share of Dutch carriers KPN and UPC. Rover attributes their success to the cooperative nature of the project, which he calls the Broadband Social Covenant. The supposedly high cost of fiber deployment, he notes, is high only for a carrier seeking to run fiber to thousands of homes. For the individual homeowner, it is a relatively small cost for a home improvement that will boost the value of the property.

---

5. Direct Competition

The most aggressive posture a community can take is to invest public funds in setting up a broadband carrier, building a network and delivering service to organizations and individuals. Local government typically takes this path after repeated attempts to interest incumbent carriers in upgrading networks have failed because the carriers could not make a business case for investment. Since municipalities need to earn a return sufficient only to pay capital and operating costs, they can frequently make such a case themselves – particularly if they already own and operate water, gas or electric utilities, as many small rural communities do. Owning these utilities means that the community already has facilities running into every home and business, as well as a backbone communications network in place to control operations.

Some communities simply decide to think differently about broadband. As the Mayor of **Fredericton, New Brunswick, Canada**[a] has put it, "we don't charge people to walk on our sidewalks; why would we charge them for broadband?" This was the argument used to help justify development of the Fred-eZone in Fredericton. Having built a money-saving network for government and institutional customers starting in 2000, the city used it as a backbone for a network of 300 WiFi access points covering an eight-square-kilometer (3 sq mi) zone, and made access free to all. The costs are considered part of the city's regular infrastructure operating budget.

Spanish Fork[b] is a rural community of 25,000 people in the US state of Utah. With very limited Internet access and no broadband availability, the community deployed a downtown wireless broadband zone in 2000 and, in 2001, used public funds to build a hybrid fiber-optic and coaxial network throughout the municipality. By mid-decade, broadband was available to 100% of residents and businesses, all schools had fiber-optic interconnection to government offices and the nearest state college, and broadband penetration had reached 40%.

Fredericton, New Brunswick, Canada

- When the carrier declined to invest, the city developed money-saving municipal fiber network in 2000

- Fiber network became the backbone for Fred-eZone free WiFi network covering 8 sq km of downtown

---

[a] 2008 Top Seven Intelligent Community
[b] 2006 Smart21 Community

Spanish Fork, Utah, USA

- Lack of broadband led this rural city to build downtown WiFi network and hybrid fiber-coax network in 2000
- By mid-decade, achieved 40% broadband penetration and 100% fiber penetration to government offices and schools

Pirai, Brazil

- Pirai Digital City program involved city, universities and federal grants in bringing broadband to rural city
- 14 Mbps wireless coverage in city core, including network of free kiosks

Westchester County, New York, USA

- Carriers declined to invest in broadband, preferring nearby New York City market
- County aggregated demand from 43 municipalities, agencies and departments worth US$10 million per year
- Cable TV carrier built and operates 800-mile fiber network reaching every corner of the county and serving 3,500 businesses and government agencies

In 2004, fewer than 6% of Brazilians, or 11 million people, were users of the Internet. Of these, about 6% had access to broadband connections, and 90% of them lived in Brazil's biggest cities. Yet, in February of that year, the little city of **Pirai**[a], located about 70 kilometers (44 miles) outside Rio de Janeiro and with a population of 23,000, switched on a wireless broadband network providing 14 Mbps of connectivity to every public facility, from the town hall to public schools and street kiosks. In 1996, Pirai elected a new mayor, Luiz Fernando de Souza, who felt strongly that communications and information technology should be part of the city's future. The Brasilia University was invited in 1997 to develop an IT master plan for Pirai and, beginning in 2001, the city won a series of grants and loans to plan a "Pirai Digital City" project. Mayor Souza's government formed an advisory board

---

[a] 2005 Top Seven Intelligent Community

made up of representatives from government, residential associations, academic and nonprofit organizations, business and labor unions to oversee the continued evolution of the plan. The city formed alliances with local businesses that could provide expertise, and with a competitive telecommunications company that could help connect nodes in the wireless network. The Pirai branch of CEDERJ, a consortium of public universities offering online courses, agreed to create an Educational Technology Center on its premises to oversee implementation. These moves, plus a re-thinking of the network requirements, allowed Pirai to drive down the cost by a factor of eight, and made it possible to finance the project within the city's budget, with only modest assistance from the national government.

When incumbent carriers ignored it in favor of neighboring New York City, **Westchester County**[a] in New York State, USA responded by developing the Westchester Telecom Network, a multi-gigabit fiber backbone that now extends over 800 miles (1278 km) into every corner of the 500-square-mile (1295 km^2) county. The county government worked with 43 local governments, an independent library system, major hospitals and dozens of school and water districts to pool communication budgets worth $50 million over five years. This long and intensive effort provided all the incentive needed for a cable TV company, Cablevision Lightpath, to build the network. Over 3,500 companies have connected directly to the Westchester Telecom Network, as well as more than half of all municipal agencies in the county, and all of the county's schools, libraries and hospitals.

Do such actions by local government represent "unfair competition" with business? Certainly. But the private sector should be cautious about claiming the moral high ground in such situations. No business has an eternal right *not* to invest

---

[a] 2008 Top Seven Intelligent Community

in a market while simultaneously preventing others with a public or economic interest from doing so.

Avoiding the Ownership Trap

As communities plot their broadband future, it is helpful to keep one thing in mind. The funding, ownership and operation of a broadband network can and often should be separated. One organization does not have to pay for, own and operate the infrastructure. This was the founding model of the telephone industry, but that does not make it the only workable model. Funding can come from many different public and private-sector sources, including barter of existing facilities. The owner of the physical facilities may not be the operator that keeps the circuits powered up and the bits flowing. And the operator may just run what is called in techspeak "the physical layer," leaving the network open to multiple service providers who pay the operator for access to that layer and deliver their services such as Web access or email to customers. The nature of today's broadband networks makes it possible to be extraordinarily creative in assembling a package of infrastructure, operations and services to meet the community's needs.

Meeting the Obstacles

Whatever path a community follows, it can expect to find obstacles in its way. Generally speaking, they grow with the community's ambition. Developmental policy favoring broadband adoption is unlikely to be controversial, since such policies are widely accepted. Having government go into the telecom business, on the other hand, can ignite controversies rising to the national level. The following are the most typical obstacles that communities meet, and ways to surmount them.

Sustainable Economic Models. Not every community can or should build its own network in competition with the private sector. No community should rely blindly on the wisdom and generosity of private-sector partners to meet the community's needs. In 2007 in the USA, there were headlines about problems with municipal broadband networks. Several well-known communities including San Francisco, Chicago, Philadelphia and Houston had previously entered into partnerships with Earthlink in which the carrier agreed to pay all development costs for a municipal wireless network and provide a minimum level of free service to low-income residents, in return for operating a paying service for others. In August 2007, the company reversed itself and demanded that cities pay for network construction. When its terms were rejected, EarthLink withdrew from the projects. Columnists bewailed the demise of "muni wireless," but the real lesson of the experience is a very old one: you can't get something for nothing. The planned networks never had sustainable business models, and it merely took EarthLink some time to realize the truth and deliver the bad news to its customers.

Communities considering any role in building telecom systems must find an economic model that makes basic business sense and is highly conservative in its estimates of revenue and expenses. Revenue will take longer than expected to grow, due to countless obstacles that will be discovered after the network is activated. Expenses will be higher than expected because they always are. No organization will do anything for free that is worth doing in the first place.

Sustainable Economic Models

- Develop conservative business case, underestimating revenues and overestimating expenses

Competitive Response

- Expect legal and regulatory response from private-sector carriers
- Incorporate delays and obstruction into business case

Manage Stakeholder Expectations and Priorities

- Appeal to stakeholder ideals (community service, social inclusion, economic growth) and self-interest (better service, cost reduction, acknowledgement, risk reduction)
- Provide consistent leadership to keep focus on the goal and progress toward it
- Focus last, not first, on technology options

Competitive Response. When governments decide to spend public money on any kind of telecommunications investment, they should expect a competitive response from the private sector. This can come as a shock. Governments are not accustomed to competition. They are further disadvantaged in any competitive encounter by the fact that, in democratic countries at least, their plans and budgets are public knowledge, whereas the private sector is entitled to keep secrets.

Private-sector competitors can respond in several ways. Legal and regulatory challenges are a nearly universal first response. Depending on the legal environment, the challenge may be offered in Council and other municipal public meetings, through appeal to state or provincial agencies, or by introducing legislation at the state, provincial or even national level. In some jurisdictions – including most of the USA – carriers can throw sand in the gears simply by filing a lawsuit to which the municipality is forced to react. The effectiveness of these tactics varies. When the small city of Glasgow, Kentucky, USA proposed to compete with the local cable TV provider, the company sent executives to a town meeting, where they told the good people of Glasgow that running a cable system was too challenging for their little minds. This bit of lobbying proved decisive: the Council voted overwhelming to build a network. But while some private-sector challenges are ham-handed, far more hit home. In May 2007, the European Commission ruled in favor of incumbent telcos that the city of Prague could not deploy a municipal wireless network because it would compete unfairly with the private sector and did not aim to cure a "market failure." In the US, thanks to effective business lobbying, seven of the 50 states have laws restricting the right of municipalities to offer communications services, and a further 13 specifically regulate municipalities in this area.

When communities win the right to deploy networks, however, there can be more challenges to come. Determined private-sector competitors can and frequently have priced their services at or below the offerings of the city, willing to risk losing money in order to maintain market share. Public investment also frequently motivates private carriers to make investments that they would not otherwise make. This is a net public benefit, whatever its impact on a municipal network project. But wise city planners take this possibility into account by ensuring that the business case makes sense even under strong competitive assault.

Managing Expectations and Priorities among Constituents and Partners. When government embarks on network development, it can be a long road. Successful Intelligent Communities create a high degree of collaboration among many partners: government agencies, school districts, institutions such as hospitals and universities, local communications and technology providers, businesses and business groups, and community groups and important citizen leaders. It is a complex ecosystem with many moving parts, each with different needs and concerns but all drawn to an opportunity to make the community a better place – as well as for some kind of personal gain. The following should be key features of any successful network development project:

- *Appeal Both to Ideals and Self-Interest.* In any collaborative endeavor, human beings have two motives, and success typically requires that you address both. There is the higher purpose: economic growth, social inclusion, building a better future, or cultural preservation. This is the "headline" that garners initial excitement and support. But the endeavor must also serve the self-interest of each party involved, whether it is for better service, increased income, reduction of risk or simply acknowledgement. In a collaborative project, all parties will typically share an interest in the higher purpose, but each may have a different self-interest, and organizers should put time into understanding the different motives and structuring the endeavor to serve as many of them as possible.

- *Leadership with a Consistent Vision.* It is vital to have a small group of effective, well-respected individuals define the vision for the project, agree on reasonable expectations and – most important of all – deliver a consistent message. This group does not do all the work: they turn to a much larger group to work out social and economic goals and impact, technology requirements, legal issues and political considerations. But steady leadership that persuades everyone of the importance of the goal – and keeps everyone focused on it over the long haul – makes the difference between success and failure.

- *Technology Comes Last.* In a network project, most people start by thinking about technology. "We need wireless," they say, or "Let's do fiber-to-the-home." But technology only succeeds when it is well designed to serve a particular purpose. The technology is just an enabler of the vision and goals of the project. It cannot overcome legal, regulatory or political obstacles. Technology is the "how," not the "what" or "why." Until you know what you want to do and why you want to do it, it is impossible to say accurately what kind of technology will do the job.

Private Property and the Public Good

The history of telecommunications is the story of tension between private property and public good. But history also illustrates how individuals and communities have charted their own creative course between these apparently opposite poles.

In 1893, Alexander Graham Bell's patents on the telephone expired. This kicked off a competitive race to market by hundreds of entrepreneurial companies in the United States. Just as broadband providers would do a century later, they focused on the cities, where a high density of customers per square mile promised the greatest profits. Yet by 1912, more farm households had telephone service than households in major cities. In 1924, the state with the most telephones per person was not an urbanized state like California or New York or Massachusetts, but the farm belt state of Iowa, deep in the rural heartland.

Why? It was all because of Joseph Gliddens. In 1874 – two years before the invention of the telephone – this inventor won a patent on a new form of fencing called barbed wire. Manufactured in vast quantities, it was cheap and easy to install. Farmers and ranchers across the US installed hundreds of thousands of miles of it to control their borders and protect their crops. When the Bell patents ceased to protect telephone technology, they seized the opportunity to buy telephone equipment and batteries. They connected the equipment to the barbed wire fences that now formed continuous networks stretching hundreds of miles. This made possible "party line" telephone systems that would become the small cooperative and privately-owned telcos which, decades later, continue to serve much of the rural United States.

It was an early example of a public-private communications partnership. The owners of the barbed-wire networks creatively deployed private assets to provide badly-needed services to users beyond each individual's property line. While American cities were just getting their first telephones, Intelligent Communities were already sprouting up on the prairie.

CHAPTER 5

Knowledge Workforce

The term "knowledge work" was coined by management consultant Peter Drucker in his 1973 book *Management: Tasks, Responsibilities, Practices*. Drucker forecast that, within one or two decades, it would become impossible to maintain a middle class lifestyle by working with one's hands. During the previous thirty years, it had been the growth of assembly-line industries that created the middle class in industrialized nations. After years of labor struggle, these industries had become places where relatively uneducated people could earn good salaries from hard work. Drucker's prescient comment signaled that the world we knew was changing. He called the new work that would be required to enter the middle class "knowledge work" and the people who performed it "knowledge workers."

In the last decade of the 20th Century and first decade of the 21st, we have seen Drucker's prediction come true. A 2002 report from the US Department of Commerce, based on the 2000 Census, compared the average annual earnings of a full-time employee with a secondary school diploma, a university degree, and a professional degree, such as a doctor, lawyer or engineer. It makes clear how much of a premium today's economy puts on educational achievement:

	Secondary	University	Professional
Annual average	US$25,900	US$45,400	US$99,300
20-year average	$518,800	$910,000	$1,986,000
Difference	0%	175%	383%

Figure 6

The Post-Industrial Economy

The rise of knowledge work, which so overwhelming rewards education, parallels the decline of manufacturing employment in industrialized nations. In 2005, for the first time since the Industrial Revolution, fewer than 10% of American workers were employed in manufacturing, according to the Organization for Economic Cooperation and Development (OECD). In Europe, the figures were slightly higher – 14% in Britain, 16% in France, 22% in Italy and 23% in Germany – while Canada clocked in at 14%. But in all of the countries mentioned, the percentage of people employed in manufacturing has fallen sharply since 1970, by amounts ranging from 25% in Italy to 60% in Britain.

This deindustrialization, by the way, is popularly seen as a symptom of decline. But it is not. On the contrary:

It is a natural stage of economic development. As a country gets richer, it is inevitable that a smaller proportion of workers will be needed in manufacturing. The first reason is that households only need so many cars, fridges or microwaves, so as they become richer, they tend to spend a bigger chunk of their income on services, such as holidays, health and education, rather than on goods. Second, it is much easier to automate manufacturing than services...Faster productivity growth than in services means that manufacturing needs fewer workers. In turn, as workers move into more productive areas, this gives a boost to overall productivity and living standards.[12]

Replacing all those manufacturing jobs have been jobs in the service sector. In 2007, the OECD reported that nearly three-quarters of civilian workers in the G7 countries were employed in services; for the 15 countries of the European Union, the figure was 70%. Clearly, some service-sector jobs require few skills beyond showing up on time and being able to read and count: jobs in retail, landscaping, child and elder care, surface transportation, and so on. Their low pay reflects the low skills requirement; US Department of Labor statistics revealed that manufacturing jobs paid an average of $29,900 in 2005, compared with $17,800 for food preparation and service jobs and $22,180 for personal service jobs.

But a steadily rising number of service-sector jobs require the essential skills of the knowledge worker: the ability to receive and analyze information, and to use it as the foundation of sometimes complex processes. Knowledge-based jobs range from technicians performing routine tasks with some knowledge component (call center operators, medical technicians, and rental car and airline agents) to mid-level and senior business executives, engineers, programmers, professionals and those working on the creative side in the arts and entertainment.

But discussions of the importance of knowledge to jobs can too easily become lost in debates about the manufacturing and service sectors. The simple fact is that all desirable jobs in industrialized economies – and increasingly in developing economies as well – are requiring a higher component of knowledge. In Singapore, the two largest contributors to the economy are manufacturing (26%) and financial services (22%). Yet employers in Singapore pay the same premium for employees with more education. In 2000, the median income was S$7,930 for university graduate households and S$5,320 for technical school graduate households, 5.5 times and 3.7 times respectively the median income of households without any higher education. Tom Davenport, author of *Working Knowledge* and *The Attention Economy*, estimated in 2005 that knowledge workers made up about 28% of the US workforce or 36 million. Other estimates have ranged as high as 45%.

Even in a "post-industrial" economy, manufacturing can still create jobs, if those jobs involve significant skills. A 2006 white paper from the Federal Reserve Bank of New York reports that, while US manufacturing has lost jobs across the nation, high-skill manufacturing employment has expanded significantly, even as employment has declined. Employment in high-skill manufacturing grew 37% from 1983 to 2002, while low-skill jobs declined 25% over the same period. [13]

Manufacturing Employment 1983-2002

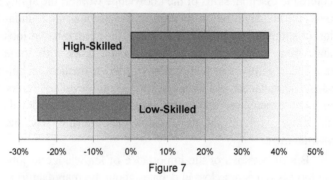

Figure 7

Knowledge Work and Broadband

Where the knowledge workforce is concerned, the broadband revolution has been a two-edged sword. Broadband has made knowledge the major economic driver it is today, by allowing multinational companies to tie together their global operations and create global markets for products and services. Low-skill jobs in industrialized nations are in decline partly because multinational companies can have low-skilled workers in developing nations do the work instead at a tiny fraction of the cost, which has made China the world's factory floor. But the pressure on skills is hardly confined to lower-wage jobs. As developing nations strive mightily to climb the skills ladder, they create opportunities to export more advanced skills, from call center operators to computer programmers and engineers.

But the broadband street runs both ways. By its very nature, knowledge gains economic value by being transmitted and broadband has become the Silk Road of the 21st Century knowledge worker. Companies whose output is information have become the global darlings of the business world, from

Microsoft and Apple to Sony, Bharti, Reuters and the News Corporation. Their information products are sold (and pirated) in developing nations and industrialized nations around the world. Google's $160 billion valuation is based on a network of server farms that map and index the Web, some smart algorithms, and a lot of talented people – not to mention the communications facility known as the Internet. It is the rise of knowledge work that makes broadband the next essential utility for communities seeking sustainable prosperity.

Assets of the Knowledge Workforce

What are the tools available to a community to promote the development of adults able to do knowledge work? It is generally accepted that the opportunity to create healthy and productive citizens begins in infancy and continues throughout our lives, leading to a wide range of programs:

Youth

Pre-school programs
Funded by local, state and national government, support working families while preparing young children for the start of formal schooling

Elementary and secondary schools
Controlled at the local, regional or national level

Community and technical colleges
Operated by local, regional or national government as well as for-profit or nonprofit educational institutions

Undergraduate and graduate colleges and universities
Operated by regional or national government as well as private nonprofits

Adult

Continuing education and retraining
Offered by local, regional or national government as well as for-profit and nonprofit educational institutions

Internal Training Programs
Offered by employers

Basic Skills Training
Offered by government

Computer and Web Literacy Training
Computer and Web literacy training offered by government
and nonprofit or for-profit educational institutions

Even a quick review of this list makes one thing clear: only
some of these assets are within the control of the local community. In most countries, pre-school, elementary and secondary
education policy is set at the national level, although the US
remains a notable exception with its tradition of local control.
Higher education is generally managed at the national or
state/provincial level, or is provided by private nonprofit
institutions. Adult skills education is typically provided by
nonprofit or for-profit technical schools or by businesses for
their own employees. Many countries have publicly-funded
skills training programs for youth and adults as well that are
delivered at the local level using money from the national or
state/provincial government.

When communities tackle development of a knowledge
workforce, then, they must do it in a complex dance of
collaboration with many levels of government, nonprofit
institutions based in the community, and local business leaders. The effort can be long and grueling, but the returns to the
community can be profound.

What Communities Can Do

Communities take different approaches depending on their
situation and available opportunities. They choose either to
coordinate or to create the educational assets they need to fill
the particular gaps they perceive. In many cases, they do both.

Coordinating Assets. Some communities have available a
wide range of educational offerings and focus on making the

"educational market" more efficient. They connect educational buyers and sellers, and ensure that education reaches not only those who can afford it but also those who need it most.

The city of **Waterloo**[a], in Canada's Ontario Province, is home to two major universities. The achievements of the community, which is home to multinational tech success stories including Research in Motion (creator of the Black-Berry) and OpenText, owe much to the intellectual property policy put into place in the 1970s by one of them: the University of Waterloo (UW). The policy allowed students and faculty members to own rights in intellectual property they developed. When the introduction of the personal computer began a decades-long wave of ICT growth, Waterloo was positioned to benefit. Like Stanford University in Silicon Valley, it spurred spin-outs of technology-based businesses, and local entrepreneurs began to build clusters of companies working on the most exciting technologies of the day. Fast-forward a few decades and the Waterloo region was the home of companies that, over the prior eight years, made up 10% of successful IPOs on the Toronto Stock Exchange.

One lesson from Waterloo's experience is that any community that is home to a significant university should learn what its intellectual property policies are and, if necessary, lobby to move them in a better direction. But there are other lessons to be gained. Waterloo is distinguished by an activist government that works to build and sustain relationships with academia and business.

- UW and Wilfrid Laurier University jointly run a Launchpad $50K Venture Creation Competition for students, researchers and community members who develop business plans and start businesses.
- Through Wilfred Laurier's Center for Community Service-Learning, nearly 1,000 students a year

[a] 2007 Intelligent Community of the Year; 2006-07 Top Seven Intelligent Community

engage with 200 local partner organizations in programs that connect community service to classroom learning.

In **New York City**,[a] the Institute for Technology and Enterprise (ITE) is devoted to building the innovation skills of people in business. Led by Dr. Mel Horwitch of the Polytechnic Institute of New York University, ITE conducts research and holds multidisciplinary leadership forums and seminars for executives and academics on fundamental emerging issues in innovation and technology management. Funded by both business and government, it has become the place executives in the region go to grapple with the complex business transformation required to pursue digitally-based innovation.

The Scottish city of **Dundee**[b] established a formal Partnership of government, business, institutions and universities in order to take advantage of a startling fact. After decades of post-industrial decline, the city began experiencing net job growth in the late 1990s thanks to its university sector. With new jobs appearing in publishing, scientific research, software, animation, computer games, film and television, the Partnership began to focus on stimulating business formation in these sectors. A government-funded Business Gateway project began providing e-business training and support to small and midsize companies, helping to improve the e-readiness of nearly 600 companies in 2004 and 2005. Moving in synch, Dundee's universities established graduate business incubators and policies promoting the spin-out of new companies. The University of Abertay Dundee opened the IC CAVE research center to support the computer game and digital entertainment sector. The Partnership launched two new marketing programs, bringing together public, private and academic leaders, to promote "BioDundee" to life science companies and "Interactive Tayside" to the digital media sector. Several

[a] 2001 Intelligent Community of the Year
[b] 2007-08 Top Seven Intelligent Community

Scottish investment programs support these efforts, including Proof of Concept, which funds pre-commercial research, and SMART/SPUR, which issues grants to small-to-midsize businesses to develop innovative and commercially viable products and processes. From 2000 to 2004, the city had net employment growth of 3.4%. That average was depressed by the loss of 3,300 manufacturing jobs, but buoyed by a 20% growth in digital media and 50-60% growth in life sciences jobs. The best news was that new business starts rose 7% during the period and unemployment dropped.

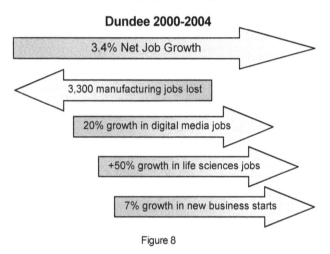

Dundee 2000-2004

3.4% Net Job Growth

3,300 manufacturing jobs lost

20% growth in digital media jobs

+50% growth in life sciences jobs

7% growth in new business starts

Figure 8

OneCommunity, the Cleveland-based nonprofit that operates an ultra-broadband network for governmental and institutional members in **Northeast Ohio**[a], works closely with the metropolitan school district, which has 15,000 teachers serving 50,000 students. The core of the relationship is the OneCommunity broadband network, but OneCommunity has taken a multi-faceted approach focusing on shared services and shared support. It has developed a OneClassroom application, which makes high-value audio and video content from hospitals and other local partners available online, with lessons

---

[a] 2008 Top Seven Intelligent Community

plans and supporting materials, to teachers and students. But, thinking outside the box, OneCommunity also established a sponsorship program that obtained obsolete PCs from corporations. These were refurbished by a local company, which had previously done most of its business outside the region, and donated by OneCommunity to the school system.

The OneCommunity Educational Ecosystem

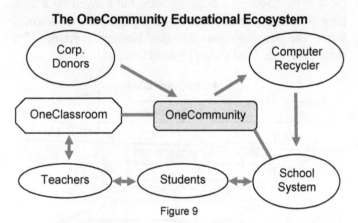

Figure 9

Through this program, the school system received badly needed technology it could not afford, and began exploring how to turn the tedious chore of systems installation and maintenance into part of its curriculum for students interested in information technology. The power of the OneCommunity network may also enable a migration to "network PCs," in which all applications reside on OneCommunity's servers. This will bring multiple benefits: lower maintenance cost, standardization of applications with one-click upgrades across the system, the ability for each student and teacher to have a custom desktop, and the ability to use low-powered PCs that would otherwise be of no value. The school system has engaged Kent State University, a local institution, to do a multi-year assessment of the program.

Creating Assets. Not all communities are blessed with the presence of prestigious universities. Even when they are, some educational gaps are harder to fill than others. In **Taipei, Taiwan**[a], a new mayor (now Taiwan's President Ma Ying-Jeou) led a major drive to move the culture of the city into the Digital Age. Among other investments, an e-schools effort placed at least one PC with broadband connectivity in every classroom, created computer labs in 250 schools and trained teachers in PC and Internet skills. An e-communities project provided free PC and Internet training to 240,000 people and established 800 public Internet kiosks throughout the city. The government has also created Taipei e-University to provide online training in academic theory and hands-on practice, leading to professional certification.

Mitaka[b], a suburb of Tokyo in Japan, introduced its first computer literacy classes for teachers and students in 1989. By the late Nineties, the city had connected its schools to broadband and the cable TV system and begun introducing digital materials and computers as learning tools. One example was a 2003 school project involving 1,400 students that experimented with a wireless network running at 52 Mbps. And the city has not neglected its post-school population. It has created a series of classes and activity groups to introduce senior citizens and parents to life on the Internet.

In **Corpus Christi, Texas, USA**[c], the Independent School District announced in 2007 that it would install an online learning environment from eChalk across all of its 62 schools. The decision followed a pilot program begun in 2005 that produced improvements in student test scores, school attendance and discipline. The online learning environment provides all students and parents with anytime, anywhere access to homework assignments, resources, grades and

---

[a] 2006 Intelligent Community of the Year
[b] 2005 Intelligent Community of the Year
[c] 2007 Smart21 Community

curriculum while allowing teachers to collaborate on and share best-practice lessons. Without widespread broadband, of course, the eChalk investment would be worthless.

Coordinating Assets

Waterloo, Ontario, Canada

- University policy encouraging spin-outs of tech companies
- University-government-business collaboration to promote entrepreneurship and engage students

New York, NY, USA

- University-based innovation center exploring fundamental issues of tech-based innovation

Dundee, Scotland, UK

- Government-business-academic partnership
- E-business training and support for SMEs
- University business incubators and policies promoting spin-out of new companies

Northeast Ohio, USA

- Content management system bringing medical and other content from community into schools
- Computer recycling program linking corporate donors, local recycling company and school system
- School curriculum on computer and network installation and maintenance

Creating Assets

Taipei, Taiwan

- E-schools program putting PCs into classrooms
- E-communities project providing free PC and Web training
- Taipei e-University providing professional certification

Mitaka, Japan

- Computer literacy classes for teachers and students
- Digital materials available via broadband and television
- Engaging students in network research

Corpus Christi, Texas, USA

- Online learning environment deployed across 62 schools
- Provides students and parents with online access to assignments, resources, grades and curricula
- Provides collaboration platform for teachers

Creating a Culture for Knowledge Work

Growing your own knowledge workers is one part of the task. Keeping them and attracting more is another. In general, knowledge workers want and can afford a good quality of life. If they do not find it in their current community, they are willing to go in search of it elsewhere.

Successful e-government programs contribute to the culture of knowledge work by delivering information and services wherever and whenever Web-savvy citizens require them. In the **Gangnam District of Seoul, South Korea**[a], about 350,000 citizens are registered users of the district's Web portal, and 210,000 are subscribers to an email system that asks for their comment on proposed laws and regulations. They seem to take their responsibilities seriously. In 2006, the district proposed installation of surveillance cameras in a particular alley in a residential district. A local human rights organization opposed the move on privacy grounds. When polled by email, however, 82% of residents supported the move and installation subsequently led to a 40% reduction in crimes in the area.

The traditional fixtures of "knowledge culture" – from theaters and museums to trendy stores, coffee shops and galleries – also play their role. One of the significant benefits of broadband, however, is that it gives smaller, more rural communities access to "big city" cultural assets as well as a means to market their own unique cultures. After building a

---

[a] 2008 Intelligent Community of the Year; 2007-08 Top Seven Intelligent Community

44-kilometer broadband network, the **Western Valley** region of Nova Scotia, Canada[a], put its county library catalogs online, creating a new local software company in the process. Nova Scotia is home to Canada's unique Acadian population — descendents of French colonists who settled there in the 1600s — and the Centre Acadian launched an online genealogy project documenting family histories, which is attracting more tourists to its Congrès Mondial Acadien festival. **Ashland, Oregon, USA[b]** is a tourist economy that is home to the Oregon Shakespeare Festival. But a community broadband network has made the community significantly more attractive to knowledge workers for companies from e-commerce and audio books to technology for unexploded ordinance.

Creating a Culture of Use

Gangnam District, Seoul, South Korea

- Email information and comment system for public policy
- Citizens comment on proposed policies and see their opinions shape outcomes

Western Valley, Nova Scotia, Canada

- Web-based cultural education spurred growth of festival

Ashland, Oregon, USA

- Former tourism economy used broadband to build more diversified economy in software, retailing and technology services

Watching Out for the Worst

In the 19th Century, Karl Marx and Frederick Engels published their fiery *Communist Manifesto*. One of its revolutionary demands was that children receive a free public education. That's right. To widespread outrage, they demanded something that every industrialized nation and most developing

---

[a] 2004 Top Seven Intelligent Community
[b] 2007-2008 Smart21 Community

nations today accept as a civil right: basic education to prepare children to become productive adults.

Public education, however, remains a funny thing. Believing in its value and paying for it can be two different things, as anyone who has ever dealt with a school budget can attest. That's sad, because the return on investment in education is incredible. It is especially so when it comes to educating those at the bottom of the income ladder, where poverty is associated with higher rates of crime, ill health and dependence on social services.

The longest running study of the impact of early childhood education in the US was the High/Scope Perry Preschool Program, which took place in Ypsilanti, Michigan beginning in 1962 and followed the kids for the next 40 years. At over $15,000 per child in 2000 dollars, the preschool program was both intensive and expensive. But its return on investment? $243,722 in 2000 dollars, or 1525%, of which 75% was estimated to go to the general public in the form of crime reduction, increased tax revenue, lower secondary and post-secondary education costs and savings on social services. [14]

There is a lesson here for every community seeking to build a knowledge workforce. It is not just about cranking more engineers and mathematicians from our universities, though modern economies desperately need them. It is not simply a matter of nurturing more of the best and brightest and guiding them into high-paying jobs. It is also about raising the minimum level of educational performance starting at the youngest possible age. When we improve the worst performers *just a little bit*, it has profound impact throughout the community, because it is those worst performers who have the power to drag down everyone else. As unlikely as it seems, one of the best ways to ensure a sound future for the children in your community is to take care of the children of people you probably wish lived somewhere else.

High/Scope Perry Preschool Program
Return on investment per child

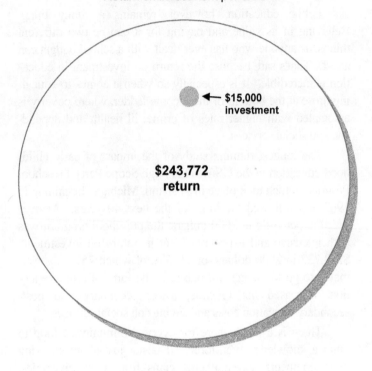

← $15,000 investment

$243,772 return

CHAPTER 6

Digital Inclusion

In the past 20 years, economic inequality has grown around the world even as economic growth has lifted an unprecedented number out of absolute poverty. In East Asia and the Pacific, the number of people living on less than US$1 per day fell by over 130 million. Yet in 2002, according to the *Economic Journal*, the income of the richest 1% on earth (about 50 million people) still equaled the total income of the poorest 60% (about 2.7 billion people). During the 1990s boom, all of the gains in world income went to the richest 20%, while the income of those in the bottom 50% actually declined.

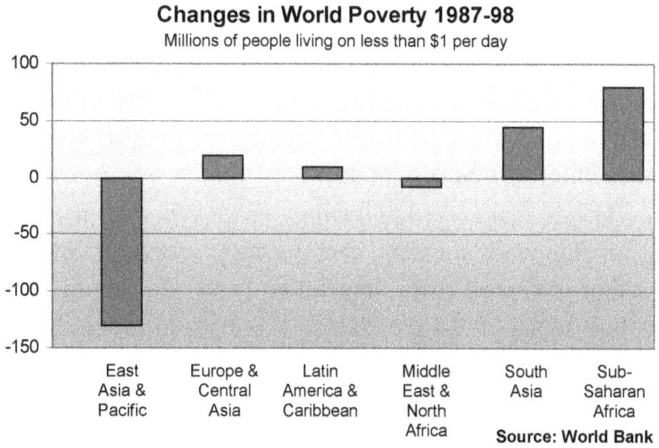

Changes in World Poverty 1987-98

Millions of people living on less than $1 per day

Source: World Bank

Figure 10

The world's story is also visible in its largest and most open economy, the United States. According to the US Census Bureau, the bottom fifth of the US population received 5.4% of America's national income in 1970, while the richest fifth got 40.9%. By 1995, twenty-five years later, the share of the bottom fifth had fallen to 4.4% but that of the top fifth had risen to 46.5%.

World Inequality 1988-93

Average yearly income received US$ (real PPP)

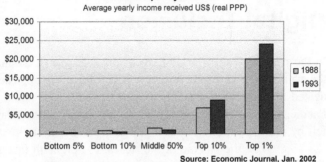

Source: Economic Journal, Jan. 2002

Figure 11

Much has been written about the growth in income inequality from political, social and moral perspectives. Amid sometimes bitter disagreement over causes, measurement and solutions, however, there are a few areas of consensus.

Income inequality is inevitable in a free market. There are few volunteers for a return to the good old Soviet days of the centrally planned economy, where everybody (except the political elite) was equally poor.

Too much income inequality is bad. When all the gains go to an elite while most are shut out from economic opportunity, labor is unproductive, innovation is nil, the rule of law is weak and social unrest inevitable. It is hard to refute the fact that the richest, most innovative and productive places in the world are those where law and custom mandate both a respect for individual property rights and a broad sharing of the economic spoils.

There is also consensus about the underlying cause of growing income inequality. *Blame the Broadband Economy.* One of its side effects has been to richly reward those who are successful in selling their services, talents or products on the world stage made possible by global communications. For an intuitive understanding of the phenomenon, think of the American movie star Will Smith. Willard Christopher Smith

Jr. was born in 1968 to a middle-class African American family. His mother served on the school board and his father owned a small company that installed freezer cabinets in supermarkets. An interest in music led him to become a successful rapper; his talent, charm and hard work opened doors to a career in television and film. But it is what happened after he started making movies that dramatizes the power of the Broadband Economy. Smith proved to be one of those stars with the charisma, talent and smarts about his choice of movies (*Independence Day*, *Men in Black*, and *I Robot*) to become a global superstar. While Hollywood has long made a tiny number of ordinary folks rich, Will Smith has become a *billionaire* just by standing in front of a camera.

In Will Smith's career, we see writ large the premium that the Broadband Economy places on skills, talents and services that can be digitally exported, and on products that can be made more accessible, customized or valuable through integration with broadband. It is no exaggeration to say that the Broadband Economy has the potential to create a golden age of prosperity, knowledge and freedom. But it has just as much potential to foster a "gilded age," in which the benefits go to a privileged few – even if they are nice guys like Mr. Smith. What will determine the difference between gold and gilding? Enlightened policies and effective programs created by governments at the local, regional and national levels. While the private sector contributes technologies and builds networks, only the public sector can ensure that the benefits are shared widely and deeply enough to tap the full potential of the broadband revolution.

Understanding Digital Exclusion

When we talk about digital inclusion, we're really talking about preventing digital exclusion. What exactly does that mean?

Robert D. Atkinson, president of the Information Technology and Innovation Foundation, put it this way in a 2008 paper: "As [we] transform into a digital society in which many aspects of everyday life are conducted online, widespread access to broadband becomes a central factor in ensuring opportunity...Whereas universal access to digital music players is not a legitimate matter of public policy concern, access to key technologies such as broadband is an important concern."[15]

The central issue is that, as broadband deploys widely through a community, there is serious risk that it will worsen the exclusion of people who already play a peripheral role in the economy and society, whether due to poverty, lack of skills, prejudice or geography. Deeper exclusion increases income inequality and all of the ills that go with it, while raising yet another obstacle to social mobility.

Market Failure

Digital exclusion occurs when some are excluded from information, services and job opportunities because they do not have access to broadband and information technology. If the provision of broadband and information technology is a 100% commercial affair largely free of regulation, exclusion is bound to occur. Some potential customers cannot afford to pay for access. Some are in locations that are unprofitable to serve because of distance, geographic barriers, low population density and generally low income. Some don't even want it, which is their privilege even if they are disadvantaged by it.

Digital exclusion represents a market failure. An unfettered free market will not produce universal electric distribution, transportation grids, or communications networks, even though society as a whole benefits enormously from them. Interestingly, the commercial providers of this infrastructure also benefit over the long term. Catherine Settanni, founder of the Digital Access Project, notes that "telecommunications companies that set prices for maximum profit and redline poorer neighborhoods might think they are benefiting, but what they are really doing is reducing their chances of expanding their own future markets."[16]   In business, however, the demands of the present typically overwhelm concerns for the future.   Executives are not rewarded, after all, for making the company succeed long after they are working somewhere else.

When markets fail to create infrastructure that benefits society, it is generally agreed that government or some non-commercial entity has a duty to do something about it. This is why governments around the world offer investment tax credits, build roads and rails, and develop seaports and air-ports. It is why, in every industrialized nation, the government has played a role in ensuring widespread deployment of elec-tricity, telephone, radio and television service. They view it as morally necessary, politically savvy and as increasing the growth potential of the entire market, thus raising living standards across the board. And so it is with digital inclusion.

Promoting Digital Inclusion

We noted in the previous chapter that most of the tools to promote the growth of a knowledge workforce are outside the hands of local government.   Where digital inclusion is concerned, it is the other way around. While nations, states and provinces do set policies promoting broadband deploy-ment, bringing the digitally excluded into the Broadband Economy is best done at the local level.

Typically, communities seek to promote digital inclusion through programs addressing access, affordability and skills.

Access
When local governments conclude that market failure is blocking some segments of their population from broadband, they respond by building networks or partnering with private-sector carriers to reduce business risk to acceptable levels.

Affordability

Computer and connections can be out of reach for some parts of the population. Communities respond by providing free access to computers and connections at public sites like libraries and community centers, as well as by subsidizing computers and connectivity for target groups.

Skills

A computer and broadband connection are useless without the right skills, ranging from PC literacy to facility with Web 2.0. Communities respond to a skills gap with training programs for every age group in schools, libraries, community centers and special purpose facilities.

In **San Francisco**[a], the city undertook a much publicized effort to provide free broadband wireless access in partnership with EarthLink, which ultimately withdrew from the project when it could not make the business model work. Interestingly, into this gap eventually stepped two organizations, one nonprofit, the other an exceptionally patient for-profit. In March 2008, the nonprofit Internet Archive began offering free broadband to public housing projects at 100 Mbps, far faster than most commercial services. Brewster Kahle, the founder of the Internet Archive, said the organization achieved the high speed by working with the city to connect the municipal fiber-optic network, which runs through the public housing developments, to an Internet Archive switching center, which in turn connects to the Internet. The first project was the 260-unit Valencia Gardens apartment building in the city's Mission District. The Internet Archive, which is best known for its digital archiving work, expected to wire more than 2,500 units in the city over the next 10 months.

In April 2008, *Fast Company* magazine reported on a decision by Meraki, a start-up funded by Google and Sequoia Capital, to cover San Francisco in a wireless "cloud" by the end of 2008, at less than a quarter of the $14 million to $17 million cost of the failed EarthLink network. Meraki's

---

[a] 2007 Smart21 Community

contribution is its low-cost wireless repeater, which it is giving away to San Franciscans who agree to use it as a node in a free mesh network that Meraki calls "Free the Net." In a mesh system, each node exchanges traffic with every other node. As long as a reasonable number of nodes are connected to the Internet, everybody can share the Web. Meraki's founders, MIT classmates Sanjit Biswas and John Bicket, cut their teeth setting up a free wireless network in Cambridge, Massachusetts for graduate students. Google liked their device enough to buy 1,000 of them for the Googleplex corporate campus as well as sinking money into the company. According to *Fast Company*, Meraki started by installing a handful of DSL lines in homes around San Francisco. Then it called for volunteers, mostly by word of mouth, to host repeaters in their homes and on rooftops (outdoor repeaters are more powerful, thanks to longer antennae). Up to 100 repeaters are needed per square mile, depending on the density and height of nearby buildings. As many as 100 people can comfortably share a DSL line; Meraki calculates they're getting 1 megabyte per second on average. As with any network, speed drops as more people log on, but heavy traffic automatically reroutes to nearby, less-trafficked connections. Six months into the project, Meraki had installed upward of 750 repeaters, covering about 10% of San Francisco; they'll need at least 10,000 – and many more DSL lines – for the entire city.

In 2004, Pedro Cerisola, Mexico's Secretary of Communications and Transport, was named Intelligent Community Visionary of the Year for his leadership of the **e-Mexico** project. Funded by the national government, e-Mexico aimed to link 90% of the nation's population to the Web through the development of 10,000 Digital Community Centers. In directing the launch of the system in 2000, President Vincente Fox set the goal of boosting Mexico's Internet penetration from only 4.5 million users to over 60 million. The Mexico City hub and first nodes were installed in January 2003. The Mexican government provided bandwidth through its satellites, and a Mexican-American team of hardware providers and integrators handled the ground systems. By June of that year, over 3,200 remote nodes were up and running and, within six months, generating a constant 24 Mbytes of network traffic during daytime hours. According to the OECD, by October 2007, e-Mexico was serving 9,200 Digital Community Centers located in schools, government buildings, healthcare facilities and social and cultural centers. The system offered users 21 Web portals on topics from health and business to migration and women's issues, as well as an online skills training program.

Cape Town, South Africa[a] chose to invest its public-access money to create a community of computer *users* rather than computer *owners*. Given the vast challenges left by the legacy of apartheid, it seems a wise choice. The UN Development Program, in its 2007-08 Human Development Index, ranked South Africa 55th out of 180 developing nations for levels of extreme poverty.[17] Cape Town's answer was to put computers and trainers into its branch libraries and to link the computers into a single network with broadband Internet access. They quickly faced the problems of success. Demand was so high that it threatened to make the system unworkable. In response, Cape Town implemented a "hot desk" management system that allowed users to log into their personal workspace from any computer in the system but also limited them to a fixed amount of online time per week.

In the vast metropolitan area of **Tianjin, China**[b], a "village to village" program has, with help from satellites, connected nearly 4,000 villages to the Internet and thereby helped to transform rural life. One small company, Jinmao Co. Ltd. in Wang Zhuang Village, was founded with the equivalent of US$62 in 1984 to manufacture manual agricultural tools. After setting up a Web site in 1996, the

[a] 2008 Smart21 Community
[b] 2006 Top Seven Intelligent Community

company began receiving orders from throughout China and expanded its products to include painting, cleaning, gardening and other tools. Their products are now available in five of the six biggest furniture chains in China, and the company's sales have reached US$18 million.

These examples make digital inclusion sound simple. But it is actually one of the most challenging aspects of building an Intelligent Community. The science fiction author Arthur C. Clarke once observed that, no matter how incredibly advanced computers become, they will still have to interface with a carbon-based, 64 Kbps system called a human being. As always in the Intelligent Community field, the technology is easy; it is humanity that's hard.

Digital Inclusion Strategies	Best Practice in
San Francisco, California, USA	
• Social entrepreneur leveraged city-owned fiber passing through public housing to bring 100 Mbps to low-income residents	• access • affordability
• Start-up donated equipment to create city-funded mesh wireless network based on volunteer participation	
Cape Town, South Africa	
• Invested limited funds in library network of public-access PCs	• access • skills
• Developed city-wide user management system giving users virtual desktops but metering usage to increase availability	
Tianjin, China	
• Built publicly-funded satellite network linking 4,000 rural villages to the Web	• access
• Internet access powered entrepreneurial growth in the countryside	

Challenges to Digital Inclusion

Every community that has addressed digital inclusion promotes the same set of achievements. So many public-access computers installed at libraries, municipal buildings, community centers and convenience stores. New classes on technology in primary and secondary schools. A rising number of adults who have participated in computer training classes provided by government-paid instructors at libraries, community centers and schools.

All are worthwhile achievements that deserve praise. But successful Intelligent Communities go deeper. In crafting digital inclusion programs, they go beyond the basics to focus on fundamental change in the dynamics of digital exclusion.

Literacy and numeracy. The tools of the digital age require reasonable literacy and numeracy, or workarounds that allow illiterate segments of the population to access online services. In industrialized nations, illiterate and semi-literate adults have two things in common. They typically remember school as a painful experience, which they are not eager to repeat, and they have learned many ways to avoid humiliation by hiding their learning deficit. Digital inclusion programs must make literacy and numeracy training readily available in ways that both preserve the dignity of users and that avoid making it look like a return to the classroom. (Holding classes somewhere *other* than the local school is a start.) Web sites designed to provide essential information to citizens can also be written on a low reading level and make use of colors and images to make them accessible to the marginally literate.

In developing nations where literacy rates are far lower, communities have developed interesting workarounds to help reach the excluded. In India, an ex-Microsoft entrepreneur named Sean Blagsvedt has launched a business networking Web site called Babajob. Babajob is for India's new class of affluent workers. It connects them not to each other, however, but to the housekeepers, gardeners, builders, chauffeurs and other laborers that a middle-class Indian lifestyle requires. Babajob invests in creating Web profiles for often illiterate people. It then charges potential employers for access to a database of prospective employees, much as online job boards do in industrialized nations. Much work has gone into making the online system consistent with Indian culture. Indians typically hire laborers by word-of-mouth, and a social networking system within Babajob mimics that tradition. [18]

Relevance. Not surprisingly, people who have never used a computer or accessed the Web may think they have nothing of value to offer. (Older adults are more likely than young people to feel this way.) Fortunately, local government and institutions are in a perfect position to change their minds. Community Web sites can offer information and services on schools, careers, taxes, recreation, transit, health, and other topics important in people's daily lives. Where segments of a community have strong religious, ethnic or cultural identity, government can work with institutions from houses of worship to social clubs to bring them online. "What's in it for me?" is an easier question to answer if community Web sites provide an on-ramp to the life of the community.

Capacity-Building. The long-term solution to digital exclusion is to have members of excluded groups – whether the working poor, the homeless, the elderly, an ethnic minority or caste – involved in providing access, delivering content and developing services. Because they are members of the group, they understand the group's needs and interests better than any outsider can. They also, it is to be hoped, have a deeper and more long-lasting commitment to moving their group from the digital periphery to the center. Digital inclusion programs must, therefore, involve a substantial effort to build not just basic skills but the capacity and incentives for the excluded to become program managers and content creators as well.

Principles of Successful Digital Inclusion

There is a final challenge to digital inclusion that bears thinking about. As your community becomes more competitive and successful in the Broadband Economy, you are likely to experience an *increase* in the digitally excluded population. When you focus on building a knowledge-based economy, you are likely as an unintended consequence to reduce opportunities for people who currently lack the skills and motivation to succeed in that environment. Programs to increase digital inclusion, then, are one means by which Intelligent Communities maintain an economically diverse population that is part of a healthy social balance.

Nothing is more likely to make those programs successful than starting with a good dose of humility. If you pursue digital inclusion, you are trying to change aspects of culture deeply rooted in history, beliefs and attitudes, with funding that is always inadequate to the task. The following principles are drawn from the experience of Intelligent Communities around the world.

Barriers to inclusion can be multiple and subtle. Success requires a great deal of input from the target users and ability to adapt. A program called Eastserve in **Manchester, England, UK**[a] provides a perfect example. The district of East Manchester – once the hub of Britain's world-leading cotton industry – was decimated by the recessions of the 1970s and 1980s. It suffered a 60% employment loss between 1975 and 1985, when 52% of households were receiving state benefits. In 1998, two of East Manchester's electoral districts

---

[a] 2006 Top Seven Intelligent Community

were among the top twenty on the UK government's National Index of Deprivation.

With the goal of establishing a community Web portal, the Eastserve project began in 2000 by surveying residents on their needs for information and their ability to access it. Residents identified four priorities: employment and training, housing, policing and street-based services. As a result, the portal design included a virtual police station with anonymous crime reporting, a home-finder system for public housing, and online job searches and resume preparation system.

The surveys also revealed that only 19% of residents had access to a computer. In response, Eastserve tapped a UK Government program in 2001 in order to distribute recycled PCs to 450 low-income households. Each household received a PC or set-top box at a subsidized price, plus free dial-up Internet access for the first three months. The project also placed PCs at public access locations including police stations, housing offices and youth clubs. The pilot was successful enough to lead to a second phase that targeted 4,500 households to receive new or recycled computers. The follow-on project also added new content to the Web portal, tied the project into IT programs for schools funded by the e-Learning Foundation, and tackled the problems of financial exclusion.

In its Phase Two, Eastserve began firing on all cylinders, thanks to the down-to-earth advice offered by a Residents Panel of volunteers and volunteer Project Board. With 25% of East Manchester residents lacking any access to broadband, the project created a wireless Eastserve Broadband network that now links 1,700 households, six community centers and 14 schools and is being extended to adjoining neighborhoods. Its work with residents convinced Eastserve that they rapidly outgrew the capabilities of recycled PCs and set-top TV systems. In response, it began offering new fully-configured PCs at a higher price (£200) compared with £50 for a recycled system. Uptake was so strong that the cost of the subsidies made it necessary to scale the pilot back to 3,500 households.

Rather than assuming they knew the answers, the project team put substantial effort into research. They carefully designed pilot programs based on the research, but did not hesitate to change the rules when further research revealed that a different design might produce better results.

All residents who purchased the subsidized systems were required to attend a three-hour training course at local community centers, online centers or the local college. Eastserve also took the opportunity created by the sale of systems to involve the East Manchester Credit Union in handling all cash for the program and offering low-interest loans to residents. The loans made it possible for many more people to participate and also connected many of them for the first time to a financial institution other than loan sharks or check-cashing services.

The Eastserve project exemplifies a commitment to identifying the often subtle barriers to digital inclusion and willingness to try different strategies to find out what actually works. Rather than assuming they knew the answers, the project team put substantial effort into research. They carefully designed pilot programs based on the research, but did not hesitate to change the rules when further research revealed that a different design might produce better results.

Two years after its initial success, however, the program nearly fell victim to its own success. Demand for computers and maintenance service was so strong that a project manager decided on a new goal: to scale up the business and put it on a proper competitive footing. He fired the large group of volunteers who had been refurbishing and repairing systems and going into people's homes to train them. He hired people and began trying to build a business. Spurned by the project that had inspired them, however, residents turned angry. Eastserve's leaders sent the project manager packing, restored the volunteer network that – everyone now realized – was at the heart of their success, and put the project back on track.

Digital Inclusion Strategies	Best Practice in
Manchester UK	
• Eastserve project created a volunteer corps that brought refurbished and new PCs, backed by training, to their neighbors	• access • affordability • skills • relevance • capacity-building
• Deployed wireless broadband network in neighborhoods where only 50% of homes had wireline telephones	
• Nonprofit program trains residents in Web 2.0 skills, which they use to report on life in the community	

The goal is not to put technology into people's hands; it is to create sustainable capacity for digital inclusion. Communities are much better positioned than national governments to address digital inclusion because the most successful efforts are driven by the excluded themselves. In Manchester, a nonprofit called People's Voice Media is using Web 2.0 social media to engage low-income citizens. People's Voice trains residents in computers, the Web, blogs, wikis, and online video – the essential networking tools of the digital age. Based in the heart of a distressed district, it provides computer labs at community centers and loans video and audio equipment. After residents graduate from a training program in the basics of news reporting, they receive a Community Reporter identity card similar to those of the accredited press. The Community Reporters produce blogs, video segments and podcasts drawn from the heart of the district, from political forums and self-produced rap videos to a highly popular blog by a local blind and deaf woman about the world from the point of view of her German Shepherd. When it comes to enlisting reporters, People's Voice is endlessly inventive. It starts online forums linking social service agencies and universities to at-home caregivers. A mobile texting campaign once asked people in three local neighborhoods, "What makes you happy?" The answers appeared instantly online. There is even an online collaborative community novel. The program is supported by the BBC, which not only earns good will but also keeps tabs on interesting young talent. The satellite TV company Sky plans to put Community Reporter content on its community television channels. And many young people have been motivated by their experience to pursue career studies in the arts, music and online media.

In **Winston-Salem, North Carolina, USA**[a], a public-private partnership called WinstonNet developed a three-pronged strategy to attack digital exclusion, with a particular focus on a largely Spanish-speaking immigrant population, which grew 37% from 2000 to 2006. In 2003, the organization dedicated its first Community Computer Lab at a recreation center. Over the next year, it opened a total of 30 sites offering free computer access to children and adults, with local Wake Forest University and Forsyth Technical Community College leading the project and Microsoft and Cisco Foundation providing funding. By 2007, there were 44 labs operating in community centers, churches, schools and libraries, managing more than 3,500 email accounts and logging over 75,000 user sessions per year.

In 2005, WinstonNet partnered with One Economy, a national nonprofit, using a grant from Cisco, to build a community Web portal. The Beehive Web portal was launched in 2006. With content in English and Spanish at a 5th grade reading level, the portal provides information on money, health, jobs, family, immigration, taxes, government

---

[a] 2008 Top Seven Intelligent Community

services and computer training and support. The library system has taken responsibility for maintaining the portal, which according to One Economy, is now number three in the nation for the most "hits" to a community Web portal.

Digital Inclusion Strategies	Best Practice in
Winston-Salem, North Carolina, USA	
• Network of Community Computer Labs hosting 75,000 user sessions per year	• literacy & numeracy
• Community Web portal providing access to essential services in English and Spanish at low reading level	• access • skills
• State-funded volunteer teacher network provides skills training through libraries	• capacity-building

In 2006, WinstonNet put the last piece in place through a partnership with Forsyth County Libraries that created a sustainable computer training program. A three-year grant from state government permitted WinstonNet to hire a full-time coordinator, who has created a volunteer group of 40+ trainers, created a standard curriculum of courses and developed a certification program. Classes are taught in both English and Spanish. In its first year, the program completed 189 classes with total attendance of just under 1,000 people.

Winston-Salem combines access (both physical access to technology and content presented in accessible form) with a skills program designed to be affordable over the long term.

Digital inclusion requires long-term investment. Because the battle against digital exclusion is a long one, communities must invest in it for many years, often with support from state, provincial and national government. For reasons of culture and history, some communities find it easier to justify long-term public financing of digital inclusion. In Seoul, South

Korea, the **Gangnam District**[a] spends substantial sums from its general fund on bridging the digital divide. In 2006, it launched TV GOV, a set of interactive e-government applications running over the familiar medium of the television set. The system enables users to access services in 34 categories, as well as government news channels, cultural and arts channels, and specialized information for seniors, women and children. To equip citizens with digital skills, a program called the Regional Information Classroom has provided classes on computers and the Web to over 400,000 citizens in their middle and senior years. Additional instruction is available via programs on TV GOV.

Digital Inclusion Strategies	Best Practice in
Gangnam District, Seoul, South Korea	
• TV GOV brings e-government to familiar environment of the television set	• access
	• skills
• Regional Information Classroom program has provided PC and Web training to 400,000 adults	• affordability
• 100 lectures from a famous private academy available online for US$21	
• Digital library offers electronic books to 133,000 students nationwide	

Education is a major expense for families with children in South Korea, and low-income students are at a substantial disadvantage. Gangnam offers several programs to lower this barrier. The district offers over 100 online lectures from a famous private academy for only 20,000 won (US$21) per year to more than 335,000 registrants. It has opened digital libraries, which provide access to 330,000 electronic books not only in those schools but nationwide to more than 133,000 students in 123 communities.

---

[a] 2008 Intelligent Community of the Year; 2006-08 Top Seven Intelligent Community

LaGrange, Georgia, USA[a] made headlines in 2000 when it decided to offer every resident free broadband Internet access via cable television. This was possible because the city operates a successful cable TV and telecom network contributing substantial income to local government. The free service was provided over keyboard-equipped televisions. As a "starter" service, it was a big hit with elderly and low-income residents but also served to build demand for more robust Internet services from the same municipal-owned company.

Digital Inclusion Strategies	Best Practice in
LaGrange, Georgia, USA	
• Deployed free Internet access via city-owned cable TV system • "Starter" Web access was a big hit with elderly and low-income residents	• access • affordablity
Djurslands, Denmark	
• Coop group pooled demand of village residents in rural area • Leased fiber ring connecting largest villages and installed point-to-point microwave to other villages, with WiFi for local distribution • Network was developed and is operated solely by volunteers	• access • affordability • capacity-building

Absent the willingness of government to invest tax dollars, communities try many different strategies to create sustainable capacity to fight digital exclusion. In **Djurslands**, a rural region of Denmark – the OECD's #1 nation for broadband penetration in 2007 – residents had no affordable access to broadband until an enthusiast named Bjarke Nielsen began a grassroots movement to build a network he called Djurslands.net. Djurslands, a sparsely-populated peninsula connected to the European continent in the south, consists of

---

[a] 2000 Intelligent Community of the Year

600 square miles (1554 km^2) surrounded by water on three sides. Yet by pooling the demand of village residents, Djurslands.net was able to rent a fiber-optic ring around the region from ISPs. The fiber net serves as backbone to WiFi networks in the big villages through which the fiber runs. It also feeds point-to-point microwave links to small villages, where mesh WiFi networks connect to still more homes. Djurslands.net is one of the biggest non-commercial rural wireless Internet networks in the world, yet runs at one-third of the cost of a similar project in an urban area and is run entirely by volunteers in several hundred villages across the region. [19]

Harnessing the Power of the Community

In the end, the best way to promote digital inclusion is to harness the power that exists in even the most distressed and excluded community. In the words of the proverb, if you give a man a fish, you feed him for a day. If you teach him to fish, you feed him for a lifetime.

Nothing could make this point more dramatically than Dabba, a South African wireless startup that turns the concept of broadband on its head. Dabba is building a mobile networking using broadband wireless as a substitute for mobile base stations. Rael Lissoos, a socially minded entrepreneur who is Dabba's founder, reprograms commodity WiFi routers to turn them into base stations and ties them together into a network using open-source software. Cheap WiFi handsets can then make calls, which are free within the Dabba network. Benefiting from vague language in South Africa's telecom regulations, Lissoos connected his local network in the Orange Farm township near Johannesburg to the national network. His customers make calls outside the network using phone minutes that Dabba buys in bulk and sells through prepaid cards. Because South Africa's retail phone rates are high, Dabba can underbid other operators and still make a profit. It also makes money from termination fees when its subscribers receive calls from outside the network.

Mr. Lissoos wants his firm to be a model for other "village telcos," as he calls Dabba. Hoping that local entrepreneurs will build their own networks and use Dabba as a gateway to the public phone system, he has teamed with Cisco to offer training classes. "Wireless networks," he says, "have traditionally been created top-down. We want to do it bottom-up." With only 50 phones connected so far, Dabba must still prove its business model but has already attracted venture capital. If the model works, it could have a transformative impact in communities across South Africa and around the world. And who knows? As Dabba customers graduate from voice to Internet, a network that is broadband-enabled from the start may become a big competitive advantage for village telcos everywhere. [20]

CHAPTER 7

Innovation

The Broadband Economy is an innovation-driven economy. The spread of global and local connectivity has had a fundamental impact on the necessity for innovation, its speed and its economic value. As barriers to trade, transport, investment and communications fall, the economic machine of which we are a part grows ever more efficient, moves ever faster, and allocates resources to their most productive use with ever greater ruthlessness. As Thomas Friedman put it in his 1999 book, *The Lexus and the Olive Tree*:

> *The barriers to entry into virtually any business today have been dramatically lowered, and this means that the speed by which a product goes from being an innovation to being a commodity has become turbocharged. If your company or country, for social, cultural or political reasons, is not willing to let creative destruction work as fast as today's turbomarkets, it will fall behind. It is not for nothing that Bill Gates likes to say at Microsoft they know only one thing: In four years, every product they make will be obsolete. The only question is whether Microsoft will make it obsolete or one of its competitors will. If Microsoft makes it obsolete, the company will thrive. If one of its competitors makes it obsolete, Microsoft will be in trouble. Bill Gates almost made Microsoft obsolete by initially suggesting that the Internet was not the future of computing. Lucky for him, he came around before his four years were up.*[21]

More recently, another guru of the Broadband Economy, Harvard professor of innovation John Kao, wrote:

Robert Solow won the Nobel Prize in economics for, among other things, demonstrating that as much as 80 percent of GDP growth comes through the introduction of new technology. And the Boston Consulting Group, in a study conducted for BusinessWeek, concluded that innovative companies achieved median profit margin growth of 3.4 percent as compared with 0.4 percent for the median S&P Global 1200. Furthermore their annualized stock returns of 14.3 percent were a full 3 percent better than the S&P 1200 over the same decade.[22]

If you are concerned with the economic growth of a community, those figures should stop you in your tracks. Eighty percent of economic growth comes from new technology? If your community is not positioned to introduce new technologies or benefit from their introduction, you're missing 80% of today's economic opportunity. (Being positioned to benefit is just as powerful as actually introducing them; it is generally accepted that the companies that sold equipment and supplies to the miners of the American Gold Rush did far better than the Forty-Niners did themselves.)

- Eighty percent of growth in a modern economy comes from the introduction of new technology
- Employers that innovate see profit margins grow 8.5 times faster than non-innovators

---

Employers that innovate see their profit margins grow 8.5 times faster than non-innovators? Since growing profit margins are the basis of job and income growth, innovative employers are the ones that every community needs.

Many government and community leaders are uncomfortable talking about increasing profit margins. They believe that government should be about "people, not profits." There is something to be said for this viewpoint: businesses, particularly big businesses, seem better able to protect their interests and promote their welfare than individuals do, making individuals more deserving of a helping hand.

But none of us can avoid the realities of life in a complex economy. Unless businesses make profits and those profits grow, they cannot invest in people and productive assets. They will not create employment, nor have the power to raise incomes. (Profitable employers may choose not to invest in their future growth, through greed or short-sightedness, but a lack of profit growth makes it certain they will not.) Business profit is the "voltage" that drives the system and makes possible everything else a community does. How that voltage is applied is a matter for debate, but the necessity for it is not.

Broadband and Innovation

Back in the 1970s, management consultant Peter Drucker wrote that –

> *Because its purpose is to create a customer, the business enterprise has two — and only these two — basic functions: marketing and innovation. Marketing and innovation alone produce results; all the rest are "costs."* [23]

Like most of what Drucker wrote, these sentences were both insightful and prophetic. In the earliest days of the Broadband Economy, he was pointing out that all the visible parts of business – its bricks and mortar, assembly lines, warehouses, headquarters, and so on – are things that cost money. The only activities that make money are performed by people: innovation (creating something new) and marketing (getting a customer to buy it).

Broadband has become to innovation what fertilizer is to farming: a heady booster of performance. Why?

- **The first requirement for innovation is knowledge**: of what customers want, of what other innovators are doing, and of what level of opportunity the market offers. Broadband has become the knowledge pipeline of the planet, making it possible for innovators to learn faster than ever before.

- **Another critical requirement for innovation is access to talent.** Broadband has allowed multinational companies to efficiently tap the world's best and brightest. Not all of these multinationals are big. Harvard's John Kao relates the story of what he calls "weightless companies [whose] gossamer scale and agility go hand in glove with the ability to exploit the advantages of globalization. Jim Hornthal, a San Francisco venture capitalist, for example, is nurturing a new venture in his one-man incubator at the San Francisco Presidio. His designer is in Japan, his front-end coding team is in Bangalore, his back-end programmers are in Russia, and he has a team of contractors sprinkled around the world. Most of these professionals remain faceless to Jim; he has never met them in person. And Jim intends to make use of Amazon's EC2 platform – short for Elastic Compute Cloud – which provides infrastructure, support and distribution capability, leveraging off Amazon's corporate assets. When a venture capitalist asked him how much the start-up was costing him, Jim said 'Three.' Oh, $3 million, came the reply. No, said Jim, $300,000." [24]

- **Innovation also requires access to markets.** You can think up all the wonderful new things you want, but until you can get them to a customer who pays you for them, they have no economic value. Broadband has made it far cheaper and easier to run a network of remote facilities or sales offices, to enforce standards of operation, branding and all the other factors in a successful marketing effort. Broadband has also made it possible to export things that were once unexportable. Just ask the business process outsourcing companies in India and China that have gone from zero to hundreds of millions of dollars in sales. They are exporting the skills of call center operators, data entry clerks, computer programmers, data analysts, and information technology managers around the world via slender strands of optical fiber. And for innovators whose product is virtual – an online service, a business process, or anything that can be delivered digitally – broadband opens the door to a potentially global market offering unbelievable rewards. It took only ten years for Google to go from what its founders thought was a really neat topic for a graduate thesis in 1998 to a publicly-traded company worth $148 billion in April 2008.

By supercharging innovation, broadband has provided us with an amazing stream of better, cheaper, faster technologies for everything from healthcare to agriculture, entertainment to education. But it has also raised the bar for everyone who participates in the Broadband Economy. The challenge for communities everywhere is to ensure that they have what it takes to innovate or benefit from innovation, because it is the new basis of sustainable economic growth.

The Raw Material of Innovation
The Intelligent Community Forum has benefited over the years from exposure to hundreds of intensively innovative

local governments. But none of them directly created economic growth. Government innovation has a role to play in capacity building, as we will see, but growing the economy is the job of the private sector.

This is an important cautionary note for people in local government. Governments tend to do poorly when it comes to picking winners and force-feeding their growth. An October 2007 article in *The Economist* summed up the role of the Indian government in the rise of its business process outsourcing industry: "In India an overbearing system known as the 'License Raj' choked the creativity out of most sectors of the economy for decades, through a mix of over-regulation, petty corruption and centralized planning. But the bureaucrats in Delhi did not understand computer software well enough to regulate it. And by the time they cottoned on, innovators in Bangalore and other corners of India had created a world-class industry." The same article went on to make a case against the creation of clusters, a favorite innovation tool of government: "Typically governments pick a promising part of their country, ideally one that has a big university nearby, and provide a pot of money that is meant to kick-start entrepreneurship under the guiding hand of benevolent bureaucrats. It has been an abysmal failure... Experts at Insead looked at efforts by the German government to create biotech clusters on a par with those found in California and concluded that 'Germany has essentially wasted $20 billion – and now Singapore is well on its way to doing the same.' An assessment by the World Bank of Singapore's multi-billion dollar efforts to create a 'biopolis' reckoned that it had only a 50-50 chance of success."[25]

As policy makers try to decide how best to raise the innovation rate of their communities, they would do well to consider the words of Bill Reinert, a senior Toyota official in North America, who told *The Economist* that "We are convinced that we are entering a disruptive future, and we want to be ready for it."[26] The old tried-and-true economic development strategies, such as targeting big employers and offering them tax incentives to relocate, may still have their place. But the rise of innovation as an economic factor is changing what it takes for communities to succeed.

Traditionally, the inputs to business growth were raw materials, investment capital, labor and a distribution channel. That's why communities have prospered from sitting atop natural resources, becoming financial centers, possessing lots of relatively low-skilled labor, and locating on seaports, canals, railroads, highways and air routes.

As the ability to innovate becomes ever more important, however, the value of the labor component drastically shifts. Low-skill labor loses its relative value, as we discussed in the Knowledge Workforce chapter, but medium-to-high-skill labor becomes of critical importance. Think of it as a new "raw material" essential to the output of finished, high-value goods and services.

In an innovation-driven economy...

Low-skill labor loses value.

Medium-to-high-skill labor gains value

That is why creating, attracting and retaining knowledge workers are the most important steps a community can take to raise its innovation rate. Unlike traditional business as most of us conceive it, an innovative business is all about people. Take software companies, generally considered to be innovation-driven businesses. Every time a software company is acquired by another firm, skeptics note the risk: the company's most important assets are people who walk out the door at five o'clock every day. Retaining those assets and adding to them – in other words, building the business – requires day-in, day-out devotion. And what has become true of business today will become true of communities tomorrow.

Building Innovation Capacity

After lifelong learning, what is the next most important key to creating a local "innovation economy?" It is attitude. Intelligent Communities focus on building the local capacity to innovate rather than achieving a few "big wins" in the business attraction game.

A percentage of small businesses are what MIT researcher David Birch termed "gazelles" – nimble, aggressive start-ups with big ambitions hungry for the resources needed to achieve them. Successful "gazelles" create the income growth on which the rest of the local economy feeds.

If your economic development program still focuses on attracting the manufacturing facilities, R&D labs or distribution hubs of the world's biggest companies, you may find near-term success. You will be lauded, and your political supporters will be grateful. But you will not be laying the foundation for sustainable economic growth. Why? Because the world's biggest companies are not net creators of jobs. They have been shrinking in terms of total employment for decades, the trend masked by frequent mergers and acquisitions. They look attractive because, with a single decision, they can bring hundreds or thousands of jobs and a ready-made tax base to a community. But investing all of your resources in them is like investing in clipper ships in the 1850s, when the age of steam power was sounding their death knell.

Where do you look instead for local income growth? To new companies. In the 20 years between 1980 and 2000, all of the net growth in American employment came from firms younger than five years old. The US offers one of the world's friendliest economies for start-ups, but the same trend is visible throughout the industrialized world. A 2002 study[27] by the Organization for Economic Cooperation and Development noted that smaller companies make significant contributions to total job gains and smaller contributions to total job losses than larger companies.

That said, it should be noted that most small companies are not fast-growing. They are retail stores, local service businesses, or small-office, home-office (SOHO) professionals. They provide "income replacement," meaning their founders' principal goal is to make a living rather than start a growth business. But a percentage of small businesses are what MIT researcher David Birch[28] termed "gazelles" – nimble, aggressive start-ups with big ambitions hungry for the resources needed to achieve them. Successful "gazelles" throughout the industrialized nations create the income growth on which the rest of the local economy feeds.

Interestingly, this same trend is visible in the corporate world. A recent report from A.T. Kearney noted that "in some industries, significant growth is still possible through acquisitions. But the unavoidable reality is that long-term advantage also requires skills at creating organic growth."[29] In short, the effort to "buy growth" through acquisition is experiencing diminishing returns for companies. The same is true of communities that seek to "buy growth" through traditional tax credit and incentives schemes. To create sustainable economic growth for current and future generations, you have to grow your own.

In **Eindhoven, Netherlands**,[a] they are growing their own in the swimming pool. The city is the home of Pieter van der Hoogenband, a swimmer who is a three-time Olympic gold medal winner. With his help, the National Swim Club has partnered with the Fortis University of Applied Sciences to develop technology that aims to make Eindhoven an international center of excellence in the training of competitive swim-

---

[a] 2008 Smart21 Community

mers. Fortis researchers have lined the pool at Eindhoven's Swim Club with cameras and used software to tie the images together into a seamless whole that can be analyzed frame by frame from the moment the swimmer dives from the starting block to the end of a race. Using the images, coaches show swimmers how to optimize every aspect of their performance and eliminate habits that would otherwise cost them tenths or hundreds of seconds.

Think Beyond the Cluster

While the sages of *The Economist* have dismissed clusters as an economic development tool, Harvard professor John Kao is a big fan. Referring to Singapore's multi-billion-dollar, cluster-based R&D promotion efforts, Dr. Kao wrote:

> *The Singapore government's commitment to innovation was never more evident than in the formation in January 2006 of the National Research Foundation (NRF). Its specific charter was to extend the nation's research thrust beyond biomedical sciences into two additional areas – environmental and water technologies and interactive and digital media – that were seen as poised for rapid growth in Asia and the world. The NRF was given a five-year budget of $3.3 billion – a budget that, taken together with other government initiatives, means little Singapore's spending on R&D will total 3 percent of GDP by 2010. Recall that the United States spends 2.7 percent of its GDP on R&D, ranking it sixth among countries that devote resources to research and development.* [30]

So, who is right? The answer can be found in a 2005 study by Booz Allen Hamilton, which was the most comprehensive effort to that time to assess the impact of R&D on corporate performance. The study concluded that "there is no relationship between R&D spending and the primary measures of economic or corporate success." That is a stunning piece of news for communities that hope to become R&D centers, not to mention the companies they hope to attract. But the news is not all bad. The amount of money spent may not matter, according to the study, but how it is spent matters very much.

The simple fact is that companies, not geographic clusters, are competitive. For clusters to succeed, they must grow and attract competitive firms, which some do exceptionally well and others do not. Simply put, a focus on clusters is beside the point. It is a focus on externals: the geographic proximity of companies that form a network of mutual support. Successful clusters are a product of entrepreneurial culture, not its creator. Clusters, incubators and accelerators can be efficient means for public and private-sector investors to deliver support services to new businesses. But they do not create and grow those businesses. Rather than focusing on creating clusters, communities should focus on the key enablers of success for innovative new businesses:

Reduce the bureaucratic load. The laws, customs and conditions of some nations make it easy to start a business, while others make it an uphill fight against great odds. According to the World Bank, the ten nations on earth where it is easiest to start a business are New Zealand, Canada, Australia, Georgia, Ireland, the USA, Mauritius, the UK, Puerto Rico and Singapore. Eight of the ten nations least friendly to start-ups are in central Africa, but Iraq and Haiti also makes the list. At the midpoint are developing nations in Africa, Asia and Latin America but also the Czech Republic and Moldova in Eastern Europe. [31]

Economy	Ease of Starting a Business	Ease of Doing Business
New Zealand	1	2
Canada	2	8
Australia	3	9
Georgia	4	15
Ireland	5	7
United States	6	3
Mauritius	7	24

Economy	Ease of Starting a Business	Ease of Doing Business
United Kingdom	8	6
Puerto Rico	9	35
Singapore	10	1
Jamaica	11	63
Macedonia, FYR	12	71
Azerbaijan	13	33
France	14	31
Hong Kong, China	15	4
Denmark	16	5
Iceland	17	11
Finland	18	14
Tonga	19	43
Belgium	20	19
Dominica	21	74
Afghanistan	22	162
Estonia	23	22
Israel	24	30
Marshall Islands	25	93
Romania	26	47
Hungary	27	41
Saudi Arabia	28	16
Sri Lanka	29	102
Sweden	30	17

Source: The World Bank (www.doingbusiness.org)

There is little that individual communities can do about national policy. But if your nation, state or province makes it difficult to start a business, you can explore ways for your community to make it easier.

Provide potential entrepreneurs with advice, help them with paperwork, even represent them before the various licensing and regulatory agencies. Convince local champions with an interest in commercializing new technologies – such as universities and technical schools – to help entrepreneurs clear the hurdles, license technology on straightforward terms, and develop progressive intellectual property policies. These are all things typically done in business incubators and accelerators – but why keep such powerful policies within the four walls of the incubator building? A community that makes it easier and faster to start and grow a business than its neighbors will enjoy a serious competitive advantage.

In **Northeast Ohio, USA**[a], three hospitals and a top university formed a nonprofit partnership called BioEnterprise to support business formation, recruitment and acceleration for emerging medical device, biotech and health care service firms. Since its founding in 2002, it has created, recruited or accelerated more than 60 companies, helped them attract more than $565 million in funding, and concluded over 225 technology transfer deals with industry partners.

In **Ottawa, Ontario, Canada**[b], a government-sponsored Entrepreneurship Center offers assistance in starting and growing companies, and connecting them with local venture capitalists. More than 2,400 clients started businesses in 2004 alone, and they created more than 7,800 new jobs and C$205 million (US$174m) in new investment.

Innovation Strategies	Best Practice in
Northeast Ohio, USA	
• BioEnterprise nonprofit, created by hospitals and university, has created, recruited or accelerated more than 60 companies, attracted $565 million in funding and concluded 225 technology transfer deals	• Easing business start-up • Access to funding
• JumpStart nonprofit provides venture capital to start-ups; in 2006, was ninth among 100 most active investors in start-up or early-stage companies	
Ottawa, Ontario, Canada	
• Government-sponsored Entrepreneurship Center helped 2,400 businesses start up, creating 7,800 jobs and C$205 in new investment in 2004 alone	• Easing business start-up

Tap market knowledge. Ask people about creativity in business, and they will tend to talk about "brainstorming" and other activities that involve throwing out ideas and writing

---

[a] 2008 Top Seven Intelligent Community
[b] 2007 Top Seven Intelligent Community

them on blank sheets of paper. But this kind of raw creativity is not the most important factor in the development of profitable new ideas. As Columbia University professor of innovation William Duggan points out in his 2007 book, *Strategic Intuition*, the most important factor is knowledge of what has gone before. Among countless examples, he cites the famous decision by Apple Computer's Steve Jobs to create a "graphical user interface" (GUI) using a computer mouse, which has since become the standard for all computers. Where did Jobs get the idea? On a tour of Xerox laboratories in Palo Alto, California, where he saw a bulky system that Xerox hoped to sell as an expensive stand-alone unit to major corporations. It featured a primitive GUI. Jobs later said:

> *They showed me really three things. But I was so blinded by the first one I didn't even really see the other two...I thought it was the best thing I'd ever seen in my life. Now remember it was very flawed, what we saw was incomplete, they'd done a bunch of things wrong...Still though the germ of the idea was there...and within you know ten minutes it was obvious to me that all computers would work like this some day.[32]*

It was obvious to Jobs because he was searching for ways to differentiate his line of Apple computers – but unless he had had this exposure to what was already in the market, he might never have made his leap of strategic intuition.

The prerequisite for creativity in business is knowledge of what has already been done. Fortunately, broadband has made it incredibly fast and easy to gain the knowledge that entrepreneurs need. So add one more to the long list of reasons your community needs affordable broadband: to give innovators a powerful tool for job creation.

Create a pipeline for talent. Improving the educational assets of a community is a big job, which can take years or even decades to bear fruit. But it takes far less time and effort to create a more effective "pipeline" through which local business can find the talent it needs. The work starts with talking to the significant employers in your community to learn what skills they need. From that point, communities conduct multifaceted efforts to attract and channel talent to their employers. In **Waterloo, Ontario, Canada**[a], a local university's Center for Community Service-Learning engages nearly 1,000 students a year with 200 local partner organizations in programs that connect community service to classroom learning. The community has also experienced a wave of immigration over the past decade and has chosen to tap it as a driver of economic growth. Businesses and nonprofit organizations have joined forces to create the Waterloo Region Immigrant Employment Network to help match recent immigrants to job opportunities, while the Waterloo Public Library has developed an online portal, ProjectNOW, to provide settlement and labor information to newcomers.

Taipei, Taiwan[b] is the world's largest producer of laptop and notebook computers and computer motherboards, and the center of the Taipei Technology Corridor, where three major technology parks house more than 2,200 companies employing 85,000 people. To feed this growth engine, the city government made it a priority to reduce the time and resources needed to turn students into productive knowledge workers. The most crucial challenge faced by Taipei's companies is the "last mile" between school and industry. Attracted by the more than US$93 million that Taipei invests each year in IT education, Microsoft selected the city as the world's first location for its Future School Program. Cisco has implemented its Network Academy in Taiwan, which has attracted participation from 79 Taiwanese companies and provided training to 16,000 students.

---

[a] 2007 Intelligent Community of the Year; 2006-07 Top Seven Intelligent Community
[b] 2006 Intelligent Community of the Year

Waterloo, Ontario, Canada

- University Center for Community Service-
  Learning connects 1,000 students per
  year with partner organizations, tying
  community service to classroom learning

- Businesses and nonprofits formed Waterloo Region Immigrant Employment Network to match immigrants to jobs

- ProjectNow portal from public library provides settlement and labor information

- Talent
  pipeline

Taipei, Taiwan

- Attracted Microsoft Future Schools program and Cisco Network Academy to
  close "last mile" from school to work

- Talent
  pipeline

Expand access to funding. While slow-growing "income replacement" companies can fund themselves from cash flow, fast-growing "gazelles" need investment capital to realize their ambitious dreams. And their communities benefit as much from the money as the companies do. Based on almost 30 years of data, Samuel Kortum and Josh Lerner, two American academics, have shown that a dollar of venture capital can stimulate as much as ten times more patenting than a dollar of traditional corporate R&D. From 1982 to 1992, they calculated that venture-capital investments in the US equaled just 3% of corporate R&D spending but produced 15% of all industrial innovations. "Venture capital" is short-hand for a broad range of non-bank, non-corporate investment, from "friends and family" and angel investing by individuals to venture fund investment in start-ups and later-stage businesses.

Communities have followed a variety of paths to create and distribute venture capital. In Waterloo, a group of business leaders launched Infusion Angels to find and fund ideas from University of Waterloo (UW) students and alumni. UW and Wilfrid Laurier jointly run a Launchpad $50K Venture

Creation Competition for students and researchers who develop business plans and start successful businesses.

Innovation Strategies	Best Practice in
Dundee, Scotland, UK	
• Proof of Concept program funding pre-commercial research	• Access to funding
• SMART/SPUR program issuing grants to SMEs for innovative and commercially viable products and processes	
Tallinn, Estonia	
• Gained European Commission funding for pilot projects in health information and remote management systems	• Access to funding

Entrepreneurs in **Dundee, Scotland, UK**[a] benefit from several Scottish investment programs, including Proof of Concept, which funds pre-commercial research, and SMART/SPUR, which issues grants to small-to-midsize businesses to develop innovative and commercially viable products and processes. In **Northeast Ohio**[b], a nonprofit called JumpStart provides venture capital to start-up companies with high growth potential. In 2006, it tied for ninth among the 100 most active investors making first-time investments in start-up or early-stage companies, according to *Entrepreneur* magazine, up from 61st place in 2005. **Tallinn, Estonia**[c] was successful in gaining European Commission funding for pilot projects in health information systems and the development of an integrated, standards-based remote management system for patients with chronic health problems.

Improve access to markets. Today, few companies can grow fast serving a local or even regional market. Hollywood, for

---

[a] 2007-08 Top Seven Intelligent Community
[b] 2008 Top Seven Intelligent Community
[c] 2007-08 Top Seven Intelligent Community

example, is certainly a successful local cluster but its continued success depends on international alliances for global distribution and financing as well as access to digital processing technologies. In *Innovation Nation*, John Kao describes what he calls the prototype of the new global company: "Skype, the toll-free, Internet-based phone service. It was founded by a Swede and a Dane who used software developers from Estonia and start-up capital from a mixed bag of European and US venture capitalists. It was headquartered in Luxembourg, with offices in London and Estonia's capital of Tallinn. From its launch in August 2003, Skype grew to 1 million daily users in just one year. Within three years, it had over 100 million registered users and 9 million users per day. Skype was acquired by America's eBay in 2005." [33]

Innovation Strategies	Best Practice in
Gangnam District, Seoul, South Korea	
• Showcases its advanced e-government systems as a means to develop business for local software and service companies	• Access to markets
• 2004 contract with Saga City, Japan	
Westchester County, New York, USA	
• Information Technology Cluster virtual corporation matches local tech specialists to potential buyers	• Access to markets
• Not-For-Profit Technology Council matches nonprofits with tech-savvy volunteers	
• US Channels Web portal promotes international trade for Westchester companies	

The success of Skype once again dramatizes the need for affordable broadband to power innovation, since broadband Internet is its sole distribution platform. But Intelligent Communities find many ways to help their employers reach a global market. Since 1995, Seoul's **Gangnam District**[a] has used local companies to develop and implement some of the world's most sophisticated e-government systems. The district receives delegations from municipal governments around the world, which can lead to business for Gangnam's vendors, like the 2004 contract between a Gangnam company and Saga City, Japan to develop an e-government platform.

In **Westchester County, New York, USA**[b], county government and business groups support a "virtual corporation" called the Westchester Information Technology Cluster. It works to match the needs of potential buyers to its database of more than 1,500 technology specialists at over 180 small-to-midsized technology companies within the county. The Westchester Not-For-Profit Technology Council provides a similar service to nonprofits in need of technology assistance by matching them with tech-savvy volunteers. Reaching beyond the US border, Westchester launched in 2007 a Web portal called US Channels (www.us-channels.com) to promote trade between county companies and the world, and has published a Chinese-language electronic magazine in DVD format.

The Power of Collaboration

In July 20087, the Information Technology and Innovation Foundation published a study by Fred Block and Matthew Keller on the US "innovation system" from 1970 to 2006. Their conclusions have implications for community innovation anywhere in the world. [34]

Block and Keller compare the common wisdom about innovation with actual practice. The common wisdom is that national governments fund basic research at big universities and national laboratories, which expands general scientific knowledge. Think of the Large Hadron Collider at CERN

---

[a] 2008 Intelligent Community of the Year; 2006-08 Top Seven Intelligent Community
[b] 2008 Top Seven Intelligent Community

near Geneva, Switzerland, which a few anxious people feared could create a black hole that would threaten all life on Earth. Business, on the other hand, funds applied research to solve technology problems and create new products and services.

What Block and Keller found was strong evidence of a more nuanced situation. They studied 36 years of data on the winners of awards presented by *R&D Magazine*. They found that, "Whereas the lion's share of the R&D 100 Award-winning US innovations in the 1970s came from corporations acting on their own, most of the...innovations of the last two decades have come from partnerships involving business and government. Indeed, in the 1970s, approximately 80% of the award-winning US innovations were from large firms acting on their own. Today, approximately two-thirds involve some kind of interorganizational collaboration."

For communities, the good news is that innovation is no longer the exclusive province of big government labs, major universities and multinational business. Collaboration has become the new paradigm. Businesses with a problem can partner with local educators, win grants from state, provincial or national government, and get to work. University teachers and students with exciting ideas can collaborate with local companies or start their own, using private or public funding. It suggests that the important work of innovation – one of the five Indicators of community intelligence in the Broadband Economy – can take place on a small as well as a big scale.

The Polytechnic Institute of New York University is a school of engineering with about 3,000 students that, in 2008, introduced a new educational model it calls "i2e." By the standards of urban centers of higher education, Polytechnic is small and highly specialized. But in the words of Poly president Jerry Hultin, "Research universities have to expand to provide not just education, not just research, but Invention, Innovation, and Entrepreneurship (i2e). And by doing so, we will have a direct impact on economic growth, jobs, and prosperity of our cities. We are encouraging our faculty to take their research to the marketplace and we are teaming with the businesses, city leaders, non-profits, and the community in creating new avenues for entrepreneurship and innovation. We have not only a new business incubator, but also a virtual incubator that has expanded from 10 companies to 40 companies. We have a venture fund for new IT and Web 2.0 startups and are seeking to create two new funds, one for clean tech and one for the health sciences. We are starting a Center for Innovation in Technology and Entertainment and Media."

The Role of E-Government

Governments may not directly create the business innovation that powers economic growth. But local government can play a powerful supportive role – by investing in e-government programs that simultaneously reduce their costs while delivering services on the anywhere-anytime basis that digitally savvy citizens expect.

E-government has an impact at the local level that is both subtle and complex. Leading by example, e-government raises the public's "digital awareness" and helps to create a more innovative culture that attracts leading-edge individuals and businesses. Money spent locally on IT products, services and support increases local demand for them. Effective e-government also signals to businesses and citizens that the community is a good destination for the "digiterati."

In short, properly executed, e-government can do more than save money and improve service delivery. It can also become a robust economic development tool.

In **Issy-les-Moulineaux**[a], a suburb of Paris, France, economic growth has been driven by a decades-long commitment to e-government. In 1980, Andre Santini was elected Mayor of Issy-les-Moulineaux. He immediately launched a campaign

---

[a] 2007 Top Seven Intelligent Community

to lure more technology companies into the area and make high-tech the backbone of the economy. Under his administration, Issy-les-Moulineaux was the first French city to introduce outdoor electronic information displays and the first to deploy a cable network. In 1993, schools introduced a smart card allowing pupils to pay for lunch electronically, while the City Council rebuilt its meeting room in 1994 as a multimedia center. That year, Mayor Santini also created a steering committee to develop Issy's "Local Information Plan." The Plan was completed at the beginning of 1996 – and just one year later, Issy decided to outsource its entire IT infrastructure to Euriware, a 10-year-old Paris company. The goal was to speed up the pace of technology innovation in the community, and Mayor Santini promoted it as the first step in transforming Issy into a "digital city."

By 2006, local government's IT and communications infrastructure had undergone vast changes. Government, school, library, and health care buildings were fully wired with broadband, and there was one PC for every 11 students in the primary schools. The multimedia City Council room broadcast its deliberations via cable TV and the Web and accepted citizen input in real time. A robust e-government portal provided online public procurement, online training, access to a "citizen relationship management" system called IRIS, and even online voting. The government consults online with a representative Citizen Panel to gather opinions on local issues, and a Participative Budget-Making Platform enables citizens to help the city in setting local investment priorities. The outsourcing contract also allowed Issy to substantially reduce costs. In a 2005 survey, the city ranked 96th out of 110 French cities of more than 50,000 inhabitants for operating costs. The population has grown 35% since 1990, swelling tax revenues, without any increase in the government payroll.

The impact on economic development has been profound. Today, 60% of the companies based in Issy-les-Moulineaux are in information and communications technology, including Cisco Systems Europe, France Telecom, Hewlett Packard, Orange Internet, Sybase, Canal+, Canal Satellite, Eurosport, France 5 and France 24. A partnership between the city and France Telecom's R&D facility has made Issy a test bed for new applications like fiber-to-the-home, which is currently deployed to a test group of 4,000 households. Business attraction and growth have been so robust that Issy-les-Moulineaux currently has more jobs than residents.

The **Gangnam District** of Seoul, South Korea launched its first e-government project in 1995. By 1997, the district had a local area network connecting government offices and a set of tax payment and other applications running on public kiosks. By 1999, the system could process all registrations, permits and other citizen applications electronically. Gangnam converted the system to the Web in 2002, and by 2006, Gangnam collected 264 billion won (US$280m) in taxes online, 15% of the total, and issued 2 million documents to citizens through the Internet or public kiosks. The system has made possible a 25% reduction in the local government's employment since 1995, saving 36.7bn won (US$39m), even as population and economic activity have grown sharply. In terms of what economists call "opportunity cost," Gangnam estimates that it has saved citizens time worth another 28.5bn won (US$30m). Just as important, it has minimized opportunities for corruption, because nearly every transaction between government and constituents (except those requiring the protection of personal privacy) takes place through Web-accessible platforms. As Koreans say, "no fungus grows in the light." Gangnam's system for providing access to public documents was adopted by the national government in 2002.

In **Sunderland, England, UK**[a], e-government has focused on bringing technology to the people. Starting in 1996, the community created what it called "electronic village

---

[a] 2003-07 Top Seven Intelligent Community; 2007 Lifetime Achievement Award Winner

halls" equipped with PCs and training staff, linked by a broadband network to city government. They have since expanded into multi-agency centers, which provide healthcare, housing, welfare rights, police, job-finder and other services as well youth and sports facilities. Videoconferencing links people using the centers to support staff. These are supplemented by kiosks distributed throughout the city. Sunderland has also identified and trained Community e-Champions to broaden digital inclusion at the neighborhood level, as part of a "peoplefirst" strategy that also equips social service workers with wireless PDAs from which they can instantly check databases and record service requests.

When he became the mayor of **Taipei, Taiwan**[a] in 1998, Ma Ying-jeou (who was elected Taiwan's President in 2008) challenged the metropolis to become what he called a Cyber-City. The first phase of the project (1999-2002) focused on building broadband infrastructure and using the Internet to improve public services. The city invested an average of US$75 million per year to install PCs on the desks of all employees at leading government agencies, deploy a city-wide electronic document system that saved US$7.5 million per year, and create hundreds of online applications ranging from requests for service to complaints about parking violations.

By May 2005, 84% of government documents were moving through its electronic exchange. Its Internet portal was offering over 400 services to an average of 3,500 citizens per day, and over 5,200 small-to-midsize companies had created Web sites on a free portal. In the longer term, Taipei aims to encourage development of better Chinese computer interfaces and expand content and applications suited to Chinese tradition. These advances will foster broadband use by citizens and provide an opportunity for Taipei's companies to more easily access business opportunities in greater China.

---

[a] 2006 Intelligent Community of the Year

Issy-les-Moulineaux, France

- To attract technology companies, Mayor began campaign to make high-tech the backbone of the community
- Local information plan led to outsourcing of the city's entire IT infrastructure to speed up technology adoption
- All governmental buildings on broadband; one PC for every 11 students in schools; Multimedia City Council room broadcasts deliberations and accepts citizen input
- E-gov portal provides online procurement, training, "citizen relationship management" system and e-voting
- Population has grown 35% with no increase in government payroll
- 60% of Issy companies are in ICT

Gangnam District, Seoul, South Korea

- Launched e-government in 1995 via public kiosks linked to local area network; by 1999, citizens could process all registrations, permits and applications electronically
- Converted system to the Web in 2002; by 2006, collected 15% of total taxes online
- System has reduced government payroll by 25% since 1995, saving US$39m
- Citizen online access to transaction status ensures high degree of transparency

Sunderland, England, UK

- Introduced Electronic Village Halls in 1996, with PCs and training staff, linked to city broadband network; since expanded into multi-agency service centers
- Community e-Champions program recruits neighbors to introduce technology
- "peoplefirst" system equips social service workers with wireless PDAs for accessing data and logging service requests during home visits

- Beginning in 1999, city provided PCs to government workers and deployed electronic document system that saved US$7.5m in its first year
- By 2006, 84% of total document traffic was online
- E-government portal offers 400 services used by 3,500 citizens per day
- 5,000+ SMEs have created Web sites on free Taipei Business Net portal

Innovation is a Loser's Game

The great and complex topic of innovation deserves one final word. As you make your community more innovative, you will need to become comfortable with failure. As Ron Adner of Insead, a French business school, puts it, "Innovation is a loser's game, as we know most initiatives fail. But the truly innovative companies know how to deal with losing."[35] The key is to fail fast. Come up with ideas, test them as fully and aggressively as possible, then clear out the failures. The secret to success in an innovation economy is not to generate many creative ideas; it is to sort out as early as possible the good from the bad and stop investing in the bad. Naturally, this runs directly contrary to both the philosophy and practice of government, in which the value of an initiative is typically less important than the degree of political support it enjoys. Intelligent Communities need to find ways to overcome the institutional bias toward avoiding risk and continuing to do whatever has been done in the past, regardless of its current effectiveness. This represents one of the biggest challenges to local governance in the Broadband Economy.

CHAPTER 8

Marketing and Advocacy

Marketing is one of the world's most misunderstood disciplines. Most of us know that it has something to do with generating more money, whether in the form of sales, increased tax revenue or more jobs. But who knows what exactly goes on inside that black box?

Marketing is the organized process of identifying prospective buyers, qualifying them to learn which have a near-term need we can meet, and bringing them up to the point of sale. Once at the point of sale, the prospect enters the sales process: a one-on-one, interactive engagement with a representative of your organization.

This is the standard structure of business sales and marketing, and the model for economic development marketing as well. Economic development officers are the sales people. They are supported by staff that takes care of the various marketing tasks that identify and qualify prospects and bring them up to the point of sale, from advertising to direct mail and email marketing, and from the economic development Web site to trade missions.

Marketing the Intelligent Community

In its 2001 study, *Benchmarking the Intelligent Community*, ICF included effective marketing among its five Intelligent Community Indicators. This may seem odd, because all communities engage in some form of marketing, and it is not immediately obvious how good marketing makes one community more "intelligent" than another. Broadband, sure. But marketing?

Yet powerful, effective marketing is vital to in helping communities survive and prosper in the Broadband Economy.

Why? With markets, capital and business operations more global than ever before, employers and citizens enjoy the biggest range of location choices in history. Just like businesses facing greater global competition, communities must work harder than ever to communicate their advantages and explain how they are maintaining or improving their position as wonderful places to live, work and build a growth business. Effective marketing is the final necessary piece of the transformative process for Intelligent Communities – the part where you tell your story.

Go Ahead. Be Dramatic.

The marketing efforts of Intelligent Communities are distinct in two ways. First, Intelligent Communities make sure to focus on selling the strengths that make them competitive in the Broadband Economy, and are not afraid to explain how the community is evolving.

Economic Development Marketing Factors	
Traditional	Intelligent Community
• Location	• Broadband connectivity
• Transportation	• Quality of childhood education
• Cost of living	
• Tax rates	• Availability of continuing education
• Labor availability and quality	• Degree of economic inequality
	• Culture and practice of innovation in business and government

Typical economic development marketing today focuses on the same business relocation factors that were important back in the middle of the 20th Century: location, transportation, cost of living, tax rates, and the availability and quality of labor. All good and necessary parts of the mix. But as we noted earlier, none of them except the quality of your labor force is as important to the success of local businesses as it used to be. Of greater importance is broadband connectivity, the quality of primary and secondary education, the availability of continuing education, the degree of economic inequality in the population, and the culture and practice of innovation in business, government and civil life. These are the vital aspects of quality of life as it is defined today by digitally savvy citizens.

Intelligent Communities expand the "talking points" in their marketing programs to cover these factors. They bring broadband, information technology, education, digital inclusion and innovation to the forefront of their Web sites, sales materials and trade missions. They are also unafraid to dramatize the story of their transformation. Many Intelligent Communities have executed – or are in the midst of executing – a shift from post-industrial decline to Broadband Economy success. Rather than glossing over the problems of the past, they use them to dramatize how far the community has come. In so doing, they highlight the leadership, community involvement and innovation that have powered the transformation.

Few communities have a more dramatic or inspiring story to tell than **Sunderland, England, UK.**[a] In the mid-1980s, this former ship-building, coal-mining and manufacturing powerhouse had an unemployment rate of 22% and was ranked in the bottom 10% of the UK's "distressed districts." Young people seeking opportunity fled south, leaving behind a low-skilled, largely elderly population. By 2004, however, the community had a 4% unemployment rate, representing a US$1.1 billion increase in personal incomes. Net new job growth was 5% compared with a 3% UK average, and average salaries at US$50,000 were almost double the UK average. The transformation was the result of unrelenting and innova-

---

[a] 2003-07 Top Seven Intelligent Community; 2007 Lifetime Achievement Award Winner

tive work by every sector of the community, and Sunderland makes sure to stress this culture of Broadband Economy success in every part of its marketing and sales efforts.

Marketing Strategies

Sunderland, England, UK

- Rose from 1980s "distressed district" with 22% unemployment rate to become regional headquarters hub and communications center

- Made the dramatic story of the community's transformation central to its marketing

Ashland, Oregon, USA

- Built a municipal fiber network that was a technical success but financial failure due to poor management

- New IT director cut costs, added revenue and turned around the project

- Made the success story an essential part of the community's marketing

Dublin, Ohio, USA

- Installed fiber network to meet municipal needs, then connected it to regional network and formed partnership with state supercomputing center

- "DubLink" network became central focus of multi-year marketing campaign about local technology success

- Deployed a wireless network on the DubLink backbone and partnered with vendor Cisco to gain national attention

In 1997, **Ashland, Oregon, USA**[a] decided to build a metropolitan fiber network in order to connect to the globe. The goal was to diversify an economy based almost entirely on tourism, thanks to its beautiful natural setting and the presence of the Oregon Shakespeare Festival. The technical implementation was so successful that, in 2006, Ashland began installing a wireless overlay to extend the fiber backbone. The community was able to document positive gains,

---

[a] 2007-2008 Smart21 Community of the Year

including the addition of 517 businesses from 1997 to 2006 in a town of just over 10,000 postal addresses. But the lack of a viable business model saddled the city with unexpected costs that rapidly eroded public support. Ashland responded by hiring an experienced IT executive, Joseph Franell, who cut costs, added revenue and turned the broadband project around. But instead of sweeping the story under the rug, Ashland has taken advantage of concern about the economic sustainability of municipal broadband networks in the US to promote its successful turnaround. Through public relations and conference presentations, it presents Ashland as a community that experienced the problems, faced them and developed innovative solutions. As a result, tiny Ashland has a national reputation for excellence.

Dublin, Ohio, USA[a] responded to the passage of America's Telecommunications Act of 1996 by deciding to build an open-access fiber network. It built a 25-mile (40-km) multi-conduit system throughout the city's commercial district in 1999, using Ca-botics technology to deploy fiber in existing sewer lines. Branded "DubLink," the open-access network sold capacity to multiple carriers, and significantly reduced their capital requirements to start up service in the commercial district. In 2003, the city itself became a carrier on the DubLink network in order to meet the networking needs of municipal buildings. By 2004, the city had connected DubLink to a regional network called Columbus Fibernet. In 2005, Dublin formed a partnership with the Ohio Supercomputing Center that gave it access to the state's ultra-broadband research and education network connecting with universities, colleges and research labs. The success of DubLink, however, was as much about marketing as connections. Marketing has been at the forefront throughout network planning and deployment, from giving the network a catchy brand name to a multi-year marketing campaign called "The Sky's the Limit,"

---

[a] 2008 Smart21 Community

featuring examples of local technology success. When the city decided in 2005 to deploy a wireless network in its commercial district, using DubLink as the backbone, it worked with Cisco to gain national attention for the initiative.

Advocacy

We must credit Michael Manakowski, Director of Economic Development for Ontario County in northern New York State, USA, for identifying another vital characteristic of Intelligent Community marketing. In a conversation in early 2008, he said that the traditional mainstays of economic development, from tax incentives to zoning changes, were "dead." Traditional external marketing has become almost worthless. Instead, he said that he found himself devoting most of his economic development marketing resources *inside* his county.

This is a startling idea, given that we usually think of economic development marketing as an effort to get businesses outside the community to open a facility inside. But Michael's observation is based on a clear-eyed view of the Broadband Economy. If all net job growth is coming from innovative new companies, and if those companies do most of their growing in the community in which they were founded, then "growing your own" is the most powerful way to develop the local economy. There will always be a need to attract outside businesses into a community, but increasingly, economic development will focus on:

- Attracting the "raw materials" needed by innovative companies, principally access to knowledge, markets and talented people.

- Positioning the community as one where innovative new companies will find the perfect fit.

Thus, it becomes just as important, or even more important in Michael's view, for a community to engage in internal *advocacy* than in external marketing. By advocacy, we mean communicating an inspiring vision of the future to the community's citizens, businesses and institutions, and also celebrating the community's progress toward that future. The experience of many Intelligent Communities bears this out.

Waterloo, Ontario, Canada was named as one of ICF's Top Seven Intelligent Communities in 2006 but did not go on to become Intelligent Community of the Year. The community's response was interesting and completely characteristic. They created an Intelligent Waterloo Steering Committee – led by Jim Balsillie, co-founder of RIM, Waterloo's Mayor and University of Waterloo President David Johnston – to raise public awareness for Intelligent Community issues and make recommendations about public investment. Rather than focusing on external marketing – such as trying to lobby ICF in advance of the next awards cycle – Waterloo focused on internal advocacy. They developed a communications program, based on the Forum's Intelligent Community Indicators, which explained the challenges facing Waterloo as well as the community's achievements. The focus, understanding and community involvement generated by Intelligent Waterloo were clearly reflected in the city's 2007 Awards nomination, which took the city through the ranks of the Smart21 and Top Seven to make it the Intelligent Community of the Year.

For **Manchester, England, UK,**[a] successful advocacy was born of repeated failure. In the late 1980s, the City Council launched an apparently harebrained scheme to win the upcoming Summer Olympics. This was at a time when the city was a poster child for urban decay that was ranked the second most depressed district in the country. Unsurprisingly, the bid failed. The Council voted to bid again for the next Summer Olympics, and again failed. A foolish waste of time and money? Perhaps. But in hindsight, according to Dave Carter, head of the Manchester Digital Development Agency,

---

[a] 2007 Top Seven Intelligent Community

the two efforts had a transformative impact on the community's view of itself. The very idea of Manchester as an Olympic site seemed preposterous beforehand. By the end of the second bid, Manchester's people saw their community competing on a world stage with the most prestigious cities on earth. It changed their perception of Manchester from a city in terminal decline to one that was going places. The small spark of hope grew into a blaze when the city bid for and won the right to host the 2002 Commonwealth Games, which drew 4,000 competitors from 72 nations in the British Commonwealth.

Sometimes, advocacy takes very tangible form. **Ichikawa, Japan**[a] developed a combination library, museum and playhouse called Media City Ichikawa. Its goal was to advocate for and build a culture of use for digital media. The facility features a library providing access to books, research, music and videos online. An Audio-Visual Center offers an expanding archive of AV material from citizens and government agencies, as well as audio and video editing suites, music and video studios and an auditorium seating 260. To build the collection, the city hosts contests for the best audio-visual work. The Central Playhouse offers children playground equipment, books and PCs as well as classes, while an Education Center is devoted to training teachers in information and communications technology. Visited by 100,000 people each month, Media City Ichikawa has been a clear success.

OneCommunity, the nonprofit at the center of **Northeast Ohio**'s Intelligent Community initiatives[b], has been a relentless external marketer. Its work has received coverage in publications ranging from *Computer World* to *The New York Times*. Its high profile surely played a role in a decision by IBM to make Cleveland the site of its first Economic

---

[a] 2006 Top Seven Intelligent Community
[b] 2008 Top Seven Intelligent Community

Development Grid project, which allows government, institutions and businesses to leverage computing power. But OneCommunity has been just as aggressive about internal advocacy. It became the Web services provider for a project of The Fund for our Economic Future, which launched in February 2006 an 18-month program called Voices & Choices. The program aimed to engage an estimated 50,000 area leaders in Internet-enabled "town meetings" and smaller-scale discussions in order to educate people about the realities facing the regional economy and create an action plan for fostering growth. Voices & Choices has led to a regional economic development plan called Advance Northeast Ohio, which focuses on business growth and attraction, talent development, inclusion and government collaboration for greater efficiency.

Advocacy Strategies

Waterloo, Ontario, Canada

- Named ICF Top Seven Intelligent Community in 2006
- Organized Intelligent Waterloo Steering Committee, led by prominent citizens, to raise public awareness and make recommendations on public awareness
- Develop communications program explaining Waterloo's challenges and achievements
- Selected as ICF's 2007 Intelligent Community of the Year

Manchester, England, UK

- Launched repeated unsuccessful bids to win the Summer Olympics, despite being ranked as the UK's second most distressed district
- Public perception changed as Manchester's citizens saw their community competing on the public stage
- Won the bid to host the 2002 Commonwealth Games, which attracted 4,000 competitors from 72 nations

Ichikawa, Japan

- Developed Media City Ichikawa, a combination library, museum and playhouse for children

- Access to AV materials, audio and video editing suites, music and video studios, playground equipment, books, PCs and teacher training in ICT
- Visited by 100,000 people per month

Northeast Ohio, USA

- "Voices & Choices" 18-month public consultation engaged 50,000 area leaders in Web-enabled "town meetings"
- Educated leaders about challenges facing the regional economy and solicited recommendations
- Led to regional economic development plan focusing on business growth and attraction, talent development, digital inclusion and local government collaboration

When in Doubt, Advocate

We have a confession to make. Some of the authors of the book are marketers. They have conceived the strategies, developed the plans, written the brochures and ads and Web sites, and measured the results. And to this day, they admire good marketing as much as they detest the bad kind.

Believe it or not, good marketing is grounded in the truth. Marketers are permitted to stress the good points at the expense of the bad, and to use language that appeals more to emotions than to reason. (Fear and greed work particularly well.) But they set themselves in opposition to the truth at their own peril. Customers are not stupid. Marketers are in the business of making promises. If the organization fails to live up to those promises, customers will notice and punishment will follow. Big powerful companies can often delay the day of reckoning, sometimes for decades, but it always comes.

For communities, good marketing is also grounded in the truth. No matter how glossy the brochure or interactive the Web site, it is not all that hard for outsiders to see the truth behind them. That is what makes advocacy such a vital partner of economic development marketing. It is the way that

Intelligent Communities work to transform the truth about their communities at its source: in the minds and hearts of the people who live and work there. When enough people in your community believe in a promising future, based on using information and communications technology to leverage local assets and strengths, they create the reality that marketers can polish to a bright shine.

CHAPTER 9

The Future of the Intelligent Community

There is an assumption at the heart of this book. If you have read this far, you probably agree with it – but you may also have reservations on the subject.

The assumption is that broadband is good for you and good for your community. Or to put it in the sociological terms of the day: that broadband Internet makes a positive contribution to "social capital."

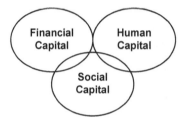

Social capital describes the benefits people gain from their relationships with other individuals and from membership in social networks. If you belong to a social club, a house of worship or a tight-knit group of fellow employees, you have access to advice as well as emotional and practical support. You also absorb lessons in behavior and attitude that help you successfully navigate through life. Social capital is distinct from a society's physical assets (financial capital) and the skills and knowledge of individuals (human capital). In Chapter 2, we called it the software of society. Like computer software, social capital is the mechanism that harnesses hardware (physical capital) and the inputs of intellectual property (human capital) to create useful output. Without enough social capital, financial investments and even investments in human capital benefit only the few while hindering the prosperity and progress of the community as a whole.

The assumption behind this book is that broadband is a net creator of social capital at the community level. But there are those who strongly disagree.

Screen Time Instead of Social Time

From the start of the electronic revolution, people have worried about its impact on society. The term "social capital" was coined by Robert Putnam, a professor of public policy at Harvard University, who tracked a decline in America's social capital over the last half century, which he measured by decreases in membership in national organizations, involvement in politics, and commitment of personal time to social and public causes. Putnam blamed the erosion on television and electronic technologies. He reasoned that as people spent more of their time watching TV, they became less likely to attend leisure activities outside the home that would bring them into contact with fellow citizens. He also attributed a reduction in trust within American society to advancements in technology. His research found that heavy TV users were unusually skeptical about the motives of others – presumably from watching too many crime dramas – and noted that people who read the newspaper more than they watched television had a higher rate of participation in civic organizations. His argument boiled down to the claim that each hour spent viewing television damaged social trust in itself and also reduced by one hour the time given to involvement in groups, thereby eroding two important contributors to social capital.

Then along came the Internet and blew the doors off worries about social capital. Unlike the one-way media of television and radio, the Internet is about interaction, which makes it far more compelling. Users request specific informa-tion and receive it. They exchange information with other users. They become creators of content consumed by thousands or millions of other users. And a host of writers, researchers and pundits began reporting what they saw as an epidemic of isolation, addiction and mental illness arising from use of the World Wide Web.

In 1998, researchers at Carnegie Mellon University reported that people who spent even a few hours a week connected to the Internet experienced higher levels of depression and loneliness. Another 1998 study of 18,000 Internet users who logged onto the ABC News Web site found that 5.7% met the study's criteria for compulsive Internet use. About a third said they regularly used the Internet as a form of escape or to alter their mood. According to the study's author, David Greenfield of the Center for Internet Studies, the "addicted" people were far more likely to admit to feelings of losing control on the Net than "nonaddicts." Other signs included time distortion, accelerated intimacy with strangers and decreased inhibition. "The Internet is unlike anything we've seen before," wrote Dr. Greenfield. "It's a socially connecting device that's socially isolating at the same time." [36]

In 2000, Stanford University's Institute for the Quantitative Study of Society published a study reporting that the Internet was creating a broad new wave of social isolation. "The more hours people use the Internet," wrote Professor Norman Nie, who led the study, "the less time they spend with real human beings." A repeat of the study published in 2005 reported even stronger evidence that Internet usage is directly related to social isolation. "Time is hydraulic," wrote Nie, meaning that time spent on the Internet reduced time spent on other activities. Specifically, the study showed that each hour on the Internet reduced face-to-face time by 23.5 minutes. According to Nie, not only does time spent online reduce face-to-face interactions with family and friends but it is also associated with lower "wellness scores," which measure psychological well-being. [37]

A study of 114 Australian teenagers published in 2005 found that they spent an average of 13 hours per week online and that one-third was in the process of becoming psychologically addicted. Study author Dr. Mubarak Ali of Flinders University in Adelaide described the addiction as similar to compulsive gambling. "Psychological addictions are caused by wanting to hang onto or enhance positive feelings and stimuli, like winning in gambling, playing computer games or projecting whatever personality you like in chat rooms," he wrote. Breaking down the number further, Dr. Ali reported that 7% of teenagers 13-17 described themselves as becoming addicted to the Net and the other 26% said they used it daily and considered it an important part of their lives. [38]

Addictive Internet?

- Time spent with digital media erodes social trust and reduces opportunities for face-to-face reaction

- Rising rates of isolation, psychological addiction and mental illness

---

According to the Center for Internet Addiction Recovery, "Internet addicts suffer from emotional problems such as depression and anxiety-related disorders and often use the fantasy world of the Internet to psychologically escape unpleasant feelings or stressful situations." According to the Center, over 60% of people seeking treatment for Internet Addiction Disorder claim involvement with sexual activities online which they consider inappropriate, such as excessive attention to pornography or involvement in explicit sexual conversations online. More than half are also addicted to alcohol, drugs, tobacco or sex. [39]

In a March 2008 article in the *American Journal of Psychiatry*, Dr. Jerald Block proposed that Internet Addiction Disorder be added to the *Diagnostic and Statistical Manual of Mental Disorders*, the official guide to diagnosis in the psychiatric field, when it was updated in 2012. *WIRED* magazine, the publication-of-record of the American Web generation, responded with a story beginning "First we all had mild Asperger's. Now Internet addiction disorder? Give a geek a break." [40]

Licensing the Devil in Our Hearts

So, according to these experts, access to the unlimited resources of the broadband Web creates addictions, increases isolation and loneliness, and breaks down the social connections that are essential to community life. But that is not the worst of it. The Web also licenses human beings to behave badly in new and frightening ways. In 1999, the US Federal Bureau of Investigation issued a report called "Cyberstalking: A New Challenge for Law Enforcement and Industry." [41] It stated that the low cost, ease of use and anonymity of the Web made it an attractive medium for fraud, for child sexual exploitation and for "cyberstalking." The FBI defined cyberstalking as using the Internet to repeatedly harass and threaten an individual, causing anxiety and fear. The Internet created new possibilities for stalkers who might previously have hung around a victim's home or workplace, sent threatening letters and left ominous voicemail messages. Using the Web, a stalker could post a controversial or enticing message on a bulletin board or chat room under the name, phone number or email address of the victim, resulting in subsequent responses being sent to the victim. The stalker could be in another state, around the corner or in the next cubicle at work. The inability to identify the source of the harassment or threats added to their impact. The report told frightening stories, like that of a 50-year-old former security guard who used the Internet to solicit the rape of a woman who rejected his romantic advances. The defendant terrorized his 28-year-old victim by impersonating her in various Internet chat rooms and bulletin boards, where he posted, along with her telephone number and address, messages that she fantasized being raped. On at least six occasions, men knocked on the woman's door saying they wanted to rape her. The perpetrator was eventually discovered, charged under a new cyberstalking law, and sent to prison.

In 2008, the Cyberbullying.us Web site published the results of a survey of American schoolchildren in the 6th through 8th grades, the middle-school years in the US. It reported on "cyberbullying," or the use of online resources to bully another child. More than 17% of middle-schoolers reported being cyberbullied at least once and nearly 18% reported that they had engaged in cyberbullying of another student. Breaking down the offense, 23% reported posting something online about another person to make others laugh, and 14% sent a text message to make someone angry or make fun of them.

Web of Evil?

- Cyberstalking harnesses the Web to strike fear in the victim's heart
- Cyberbullying unleashes psychological damage on youngsters
- Sexual predators stalk the Web looking for victims

Of all the concerns about bad actors on the Web, fear of sexual predators tops the list. American parents have been terrorized by statistics from two studies conducted by the Crimes Against Children Research Center, which claim that "one in five youth have been sexually solicited online." Dark images of predators waiting to trap unwary children using the Web fill parental magazines and Web sites. As with cyberstalking and cyberbullying, the anonymity provided by the Web raises the fear level to unprecedented heights.

Adapting to "the New"

If you take this wave of research at face value, the conclusion is clear. The Web is a destroyer of social capital. Power it up with broadband, and you have the makings of a virtual plague laying waste your community.

But is it so?

For a different point of view, consider educator and attorney Nancy Willard, who writes for the Education World Web site (www.education-world.com). She notes that the Crimes Against Children Research Center studies asked teens to report on "any situation where someone on the Internet attempted to get them to talk about sex when they did not want to or asked them unwanted sexual questions about themselves." As Ms. Willard wryly asks, "Now, you tell me how often that happens in middle and high schools every day." In the Center studies, she notes, 43-48% of the "sexual solicitors" were thought to be other teens. Twenty to thirty percent were thought to be between 18 and 25, and only 4 percent over 25. More significantly, 70% of the young people in the studies indicated that the solicitation did not make them feel upset or afraid. Another study by the Center revealed that deception about sexual motivations is rare online. In cases of actual arrests where teens met in person with an online sexual predator, "the offenders openly sexually solicited the victims. The victims knew they were interacting with men who were interested in them sexually. The victims went willingly with the offender and most met with the offender more than once. After the arrest, half the victims described themselves as in love with, or good friends with, the offender." [42]

In 2007, Britain's Prime Minister asked psychologist and parenting expert Dr. Tanya Byron to conduct an independent review of the risks of exposing children to sex and violence on the Internet and in video games. Her report noted that the digital divide between generations made parents feel ill-equipped to help their children, which in turn led to fear and a sense of helplessness. In addition to recommending that rating systems be improved to give parents more information, she had this to say: "Children will be children – pushing boundaries and taking risks. At a public swimming pool we have gates, put up signs, have lifeguards and shallow ends, but we also teach children how to swim."

In a word, all of these baleful behaviors are *familiar*. We have seen them before, and we should not be surprised to see them again in the virtual world of the Web. Any technology that gives more scope to the human capacity for folly and evil is bad. But then, so are airplane crashes.

We think that these level-headed responses cut to the core of the concerns about the Web's impact on social capital. The Web appears to expand *slightly* the scope for human behavior with bad, even horrible consequences: obsession and compulsion, neurosis and psychosis, fear, jealousy, hatred, the lust for vengeance, and the desire to dominate. The human capacity for addictive behavior is triggered not only by drugs but by a wide range of experiences from gambling to shopping to television. Yet pathological gamblers are pathological whether they gamble online or in a casino. People with sexual obsessions are obsessive regardless of whether the pornography is viewed online or on paper, and an obsessive shopper does not need e-commerce to run up huge credit card bills. Dr. Block's proposal to make Internet Addiction Disorder a standard diagnosis has run into steady criticism from colleagues who believe that excessive Internet use is no more than a symptom of already well-known disorders.

"New" categories of misbehavior like cyberstalking and cyberbullying seem to fit the same pattern. The Web adds one more tool to the arsenal of the stalker but does not fundamentally change the nature of the behavior. It has challenged law enforcement to define new crimes so that perpetrators do not escape justice, but the new criminal codes are extensions of existing ones. As for cyberbullying and online sexual predation, they are re-creations in cyberspace of the kinds of behavior that good parents, schools and communities have long sought to control in real life.

In a word, all of these baleful behaviors are *familiar*. We have seen them before, and we should not be surprised to see them again in the virtual world of the Web. Any technology that gives more scope to the human capacity for folly and evil is bad. But then, so are airplane crashes. Rather than outlawing air travel, however, we have worked so hard and well to make it safe that you are far more likely to die in your car than in an airliner. The same thing is happening online. All of the research studies and conferences and articles can be seen as a conversation we are having with ourselves about how to adapt to these virtual extensions of real life. And adapt we are, by passing new laws, teaching our children and ourselves safe use of the Web, and developing systems to protect the security of, for example, credit card numbers transmitted over the Internet.

What's most revealing about this process is the way we apply old ways of thinking to new developments. When we think about how the Web is transforming our lives, we focus on the negatives, because we *recognize* them. We blame the technology for the changes rather than seeing them as natural extensions of existing problems into the new environment of the Web. When the automobile became a common household possession, it was blamed for fostering moral turpitude. Instead of courting politely in full view of their parents, young people could speed off to secluded destinations, there to engage in who knew what. It was the car that was to blame – not the fact that youngsters had yearned for such freedom since the beginning of civilization.

What we seldom see – because we do not yet have a mental framework for understanding – are the new ways in which the Web is making a positive contribution to social capital at the community level.

Community Online or Online Community?

In 2003-04, NetLab – which is a project of the Center for Urban and Community Studies at the University of Toronto – studied the impact of the Web on a mid-priced housing development near Toronto that provided broadband to most homes at 10 Mbits per second. The research sought to learn how living in "Netville," as it dubbed the community, affected people's community relations, online and offline, in the neighborhood and far away. The results suggested that high-speed Internet access supports rather than weakens neighborhood bonds. Wired residents had much more informal contact with neighbors than did non-wired residents. They knew the names of 25 neighbors compared with an average of 8 for non-wired residents, and made 50% more visits to each other's homes. Their contacts with neighbors were also more dispersed throughout the housing development rather than being restricted to next-door neighbors. At the same time, wired Netville residents maintained more long-distance contact with friends and relatives than non-wired residents. In short, broadband enabled residents to create more meaningful relationships with members of their geographical community while at the same time maintaining relationships with distant friends and relations. [43]

NetLab also collaborated with the National Geographic Survey 2000, which sought to characterize Web users across North America. The survey found that, rather than weakening community, the Internet supplements existing face-to-face and telephone contact. Heavy Internet users had a greater overall volume of contact with community members; frequent contact via the Internet was associated with frequent contact via other means. NetLab's conclusion was that the Internet is not a self-contained online world. Rather than operating at the expense of reality, the Web has become part of it, with people using all means of communications to connect with friends and relatives. Communities both physical and virtual are integrating the Web into the regular patterns of social life. [44]

Another Canadian study from the University of Moncton challenged the notion that Internet use automatically detracts from family life. It tracked the person-to-person impact of introducing broadband into a rural community in rural Atlantic Canada. Over 80% of respondents said that they spent the same time together as a family following the introduction of broadband as beforehand, while gaining significant new capabilities, from online banking and shopping to collaboration on school projects and tracking investments. [45]

Part of the Physical World

- "Wired" residents of "Netville" knew the names of 25 neighbors (compared with 8 for non-wired residents) and made 50% more visits to each other's homes
- Heavy Internet users have a greater overall volume of contact with community members
- Rather than operating at the expense of the physical world, the Web has become part of it
- After introduction of broadband, 80% of rural residents said they spent the same time together as a family as they had previously done

---

How can this be? The reasoning of Robert Putnam and Norman Nie seems unassailable: time spent online is time no longer available for face-to-face involvement in family, friends and the life of the community. Is time not really "hydraulic," as Nie said of it?

Not really. What Putnam and Nie failed to notice is the power of the Web to let us to more in less time – that is, to be more efficient. Time spent online is not necessarily time taken from family, friends and community. It can just as easily be time taken from standing in line at the bank, dazed hours spent wandering the shopping mall, evening devoted to television or newspaper, weekends spent comparison shopping for cars, appliances and other major purchases, time spent researching health issues, managing investments or finding advice and support for everything from hobbies to emotional problems.

In October 2001, the Pew Internet & American Life project published a seminal study on "networks that nurture long-distance relationships and local ties." Keeping in mind that the findings relate specifically to Americans rather than being global, they were striking in particular for how early in the development of the Web they were reported. In 2001, according to Pew:

- 84% of Internet users, or about 90 million Americans, said they had used the Internet to contact or get information from a group. The study termed them "Cyber Groupies."

- 79% of Cyber Groupies identified at least one group with which they stayed in regular contact.

- 40% of Cyber Groupies said the Internet helped them become more involved with groups to which they already belonged.

- 26% of all Internet users (28 million people) had employed the Internet to connect with local groups. The study termed them "Local Groupies."

- 33% of the 28 million Local Groupies sent email several times a week to their main local organization, which included religious, social and charitable organizations as well as community, neighborhood, youth and local sports groups.

- 41% of all Internet users said they "often" or "sometimes" went online to seek information about local stores or merchants.

- 35% of all Internet users "often" or "sometimes" went online for news about the local community.

The study concluded that online communities had become "virtual third places" for people, different from home or work, with boundaries that spanned from the local community to global interest groups. Study author John Horrigan also noted that young people were much more likely than other users to report that the Internet had helped them become more involved in community organizations as well as connect with people of different generations, economic backgrounds and ethnic groups. The primary draw to online communities for young people appeared to be hobby groups but a secondary outcome, as they surfed to other online communities, was to connect many to groups that helped foster civic engagement. [46]

Building Social Capital Online

Seven years later in 2008, Don Tapscott published *Grown Up Digital: How the Net Generation is Changing Your World.* It described today's "Net Generation" as "smarter, quicker and more tolerant of diversity than their predecessors." As demonstrated in the Obama presidential campaign, "these empowered young people are beginning to transform every institution of modern life."

Mr. Tapscott believes that the experience of parents who grew up watching television is misleading when it comes to judging the 20,000 hours on the Internet and 10,000 hours playing video games spent by a typical 20-year-old American today. "The Net Generation is in many ways the antithesis of the TV generation," he writes. Rather than "leaning back" on the couch as passive consumers of media, they "lean forward" to interact, choose and challenge.[47]

In November 2008, the MacArthur Foundation published the results of the Digital Youth Project, a 3-year ethnographic study of how young people actually use new media. They found that kids use social network sites, online games, video-sharing sites and mobile phones to connect with peers in new ways, yet to serve needs that are as old as time. "While the pace of technological change may seem dizzying," says the report, "the underlying practices of sociability, learning, play and self-expression are undergoing a slower evolution, growing out of resilient social and cultural structures." [48]

Most kids use online networks to extend the friendships they already have in school, religious organizations and sports. In what the report called these "friendship-driven" practices, the kids are essentially "hanging out" online, as they would otherwise do at school, the mall, home or street. "Hanging out" may seem a waste of time, if not downright worrisome, to adults. But it is clearly an exercise that builds bonds in the community and engages young people in local culture.

A smaller number of young people also use the online world to explore interests that go beyond what they can access locally. Online groups allow youth to find and connect with peers who share specialized interests, from online gaming to creative writing to video editing. Much of what they learn comes from their peers rather than recognized adult authorities, but where adults do engage them – as when 30-year-olds play online games – the adult leadership frequently becomes central to a collaboration through which users define standards for expertise in the field.

In both cases, the study insists that youth are picking up basic social and technological skills that they need to fully participate in today's society. They are building a shared understanding of how to present themselves online and how to manage relationships in the online world. In the process, they are developing, in addition to habits that bewilder their parents, new genres of written and multimedia communication.

The work of these social scientists is shedding new light on the relationship between broadband and community development. It is beginning to tease out how people actually use broadband-based technologies – as opposed to how we *think* they use them – and finding that their primary goal is to slake a deep thirst for community, whether based on shared geography or on shared interests.

From the Internet's earliest days, the "killer app" has been personal communications, otherwise known as email, and the trend has only accelerated in the 21st Century. At the end of 2008, the social networking site Facebook had more than 140 million active users, while in October of that year, its business and professional counterpart, LinkedIn, reported 30 million users in 150 countries and growth at the rate of half a million new members per week.[49] Meanwhile, newer platforms like Twitter, which had 200,000 active users sending 3 million messages daily in March 2008, continue to expand the toolkit of the digitally connected.[50]

If the results of the Digital Youth Project apply to the population at large, most people today are using these digital interactions to overlay and extend the physical realm. For them, the Web is increasingly providing a digital projection of life as it is lived within the community, and an on-ramp to deeper engagement in it.

An Unregulated Sanctuary

An extreme case of the Web contributing to civic engagement by the young was reported by Jongwoo Han in the Maxwell School of Citizenship and Public Affairs at Syracuse University. He analyzed the impact of the Internet on the growth of social capital and democracy in South Korea, one of the world's broadband leaders, from 2000 to 2002. Politics in South Korea has traditionally been a "top down" process, with the state exercising almost total control over civil society. That tradition began to collapse in the late 1980s when civic activism brought military rule to an end and put into place the early stages of democratic governance.

Han traces the 700% growth of Internet penetration from 1999, when 3 million people were Internet users, to 2001, when 24 million South Koreans were online. As elsewhere in the world, penetration skewed sharply by age. In 2001, the Internet penetration rate reached 93% among 7-19 year olds and 85% among people in their 20s, compared with 36% for people in their 40s and 9% for people in their 50s. Unlike most places, however, the Internet boom coincided with dramatic breakthroughs in civic participation. It first became apparent in the 2000 National Assembly election, when the Citizens' Council for Economic Justice, the nation's largest civic organization, published on its Web site a list of 164 candidates it considered unfit for public office due to past corruption, suspect voting records and unethical behavior. Of the 164, the Council specifically targeted 86 incumbents for defeat. The Council's list appeared on numerous civic Web sites that, within five days of publication, attracted 50,000 visitors. And of the 86 incumbents targeted online, 69% went down to defeat in the April 13 election.

The feat was repeated in the December 2002 presidential election. Roh Moo-Hyun, who was to become South Korea's president, held a very narrow lead over his opponent. When political maneuvering by his opponents made it appear that Roh would lose, his Internet fan club orchestrated a last-minute mobilization of young voters. During an 8-hour period from 10 pm on December 18 until the vote the following morning, Roh's supporters rallied using instant messaging and cell phone texting. News sites experienced traffic that was five times their daily average, which in some cases crashed their servers. Visitors to the ruling party's Web site recorded over 860,000 hits, 200,000 more than the daily average, and postings on bulletin boards doubled. Roh's narrow 560,000-vote margin of victory was largely attributed to voters under

30, who preferred him by nearly 2 to 1 and who also had the nation's highest Internet penetration rate.

How Roh Moo-hyun Became President

- Political maneuvering in December 2002 election made it appear likely that Roh, who held a narrow lead, would lose
- Supporters organized a last-minute mobilization during an 8-hour period on election day, using instant messaging, mobile phone texting and the Web
- Hits to political Web sites and chat rooms skyrocketed
- Roh's 560,000-vote margin of victory was attributed to voters under 30, who preferred him by nearly 2 to 1 and who had the nation's highest Internet penetration rate

---

Han credits two particular aspects of the Web – which others consider to be its primary faults – for this outcome. The first is anonymity. In a society regulated by powerful traditions, the Web offered young people a "socially unregulated sanctuary of diverse opinions and interests." The second is the low cost of entry. "Getting public attention depends upon the content of the Web site," Han wrote. "Gatekeepers such as editors, publishers, newspapers and political parties have significantly lost their regulating power." [51]

The Future May Not Look Like the Past

In 1996, the following conversation took place between two senior executives at a communications industry trade show. One asked the other, "This Internet thing. Think there's anything in it?"

At about the same time, a top telecom consultant – one with decades of experience at British Telecom, who went on to take the lead role in writing the regulations that privatized South Africa Telekom – predicted that the Internet was doomed to failure. It had no commercial basis, he explained, just carriers bartering traffic with each other and nobody paying realistic prices for anything.

No, these men weren't fools. It was just 1996. The Web had proven its immense global popularity but there was little hard evidence that it offered any meaningful economic proposition. Here in the new century's first decade, with companies from Google to eBay to Amazon.com having achieved great success, there is no longer any doubt.

We believe that the same holds true of the Intelligent Community. The concept remains new. The synergy among broadband, knowledge work, digital inclusion, innovation, marketing and advocacy is clear to some but certainly remains unproven. What does seem certain is that Intelligent Communities will continue to evolve in ways that can hardly be guessed at. We believe that the broadband Web will not only contribute to their economic growth but will also create and nurture their social capital. Communities that neglect broadband infrastructure and that fail to improve education, engage the disadvantaged, spur innovation or market themselves well will face even greater threats to their sustainability in the future. And when we speak of the future, we know one thing.

It's all about the children.

The Intelligent Community Forum

More information on the communities cited in this book is available at the Web site of the Intelligent Community Forum (www.intelligentcommunity.org).

ICF is a think tank that focuses on the creation of inclusive and sustainable economic growth in the Broadband Economy. Our area of interest is the local community, both large and small, in the developing and developed economies of the world. ICF conducts research, creates conference content, publishes information and presents annual awards, all in an effort to:

- Identify and explain the emergence of the broadband economy and its impact at the local level.

- Research and share best practices by communities in adapting to the changing economic environment and positioning their citizens and businesses to prosper.

- Celebrate the achievements of communities that have overcome challenges to claim a place in the economy of the 21st century.

The Intelligent Community Forum is known for its international Awards program, which names the Smart21, the Top Seven and the Intelligent Community of the Year. Each year's Awards program begins in June, when we receive nominations from hundreds of communities (www.intelligentcommunity.org/nominations) around the world. In October, we name a select group of them as our

Smart21 Communities of the Year. In January, we narrow this group to the Top Seven Intelligent Communities, based on quantitative review of detailed data submitted by the Smart21. Finally, in May, after site visits to each of the Top Seven, we name one as the Intelligent Community of the Year. At each stage, the communities receive substantial press coverage for their achievements, and often use this acknowledgement as a means to build support for continued change among citizens, businesses and institutions.

Support the Forum

The Awards program is also an ongoing research project. From information provided by communities, we identify and document best practices in broadband deployment, knowledge workforce development, digital inclusion, innovation and economic development marketing and advocacy. We then share this information with communities around the world, in order to help them meet the challenges of the Broadband Economy. Our work helps:

- Steer communities onto the path of sustainable and inclusive economic growth

- Invigorate entrepreneurship and the creation of knowledge economies at the local level

- Reduce the economic inequality that leads to social dysfunction

- Prevent the "brain drain" of young talent that dooms communities to stagnation

- Empower communities to re-energize local culture and give it new economic expression

- Promote greater citizen participation and greater transparency and accountability in government

Your contributions to ICF support our Awards program, the Building the Broadband Economy summit, the annual ICF Immersion Lab study tour of Intelligent Communities, and our research programs.

Intelligent Community Forum

55 Broad Street, 14th Floor, New York, NY 10004 USA

+1 646-291-6166   www.intelligentcommunity.org

Index

Notes

[1] Th. Brinkhoff: The Principal Agglomerations of the World, http://www.citypopulation.de, 2007-09-30

[2] "Who's Ahead in Global Manufacturing Output?" by Joseph Quinlan, *The Globalist* (www.theglobalist.com), September 6, 2005.

[3] "Offshoring's Impact On Future Tech Jobs Is Overrated, Says Study" By Marianne Kolbasuk McGee, ChannelWeb (www.channelweb.com), February 23, 2006

[4] *The World is Flat* by Thomas L. Friedman, Farrar Straus and Giroux, 2005

[5] "World Broadband Lines Reach 111.7m in Q1 2004," PointTopic, June 23, 2004.

[6] International Telecommunications Union ICT Statistics Database

[7] Ibid

[8] "Africa Calling," *The Economist*, June 5, 2008

[9] "Cash on Call" by Tom Standage, *The Economist World in Print 2008*

[10] "The Digital Provide: Information (Technology), Market Performance and Welfare in the South Indian Fisheries Sector" by Robert Jensen, *Quarterly Journal of Economics*, August 2007.

[11] "To Do With the Price of Fish," *The Economist*, May 10, 2007

[12] "Industrial Metamorphosis," *The Economist*, 29 September 2005.

[13] "A Leaner, More Skilled US Manufacturing Workforce," Richard Deitz and James Orr, Current Issues in *Economics and Finance*, Volume 12, Number 2, February/March 2006, The Federal Reserve Bank of New York

[14] *Dollars and Sense: A Review of Economic Analyses of Pre-K*, PreK Now, May 2007.

[15] "Framing a National Broadband Policy" by Robert D. Atkinson, *CommLaw Conspectus*, January 18, 2008.

[16] Quoted in "What Are the Barriers to Digital Inclusion?" by Sascha Meinrath, *Government Technology*, November 20, 2006.

[17] Human Development Report 2007-08, United Nations Development Program (http://hdrstats.undp.org)

[18] "In India, Poverty Inspires Technology Workers to Altruism" by Anand Giridharadas, *The New York Times*, October 30, 2007

[19] "Djurlands.Net: A Wireless Project Where Sharing Knowledge, Not Technology, Matters Most" by Indrajit Basu, *Digital Communities*, Jun 1, 2007

[20] "Yabba Dabba Do," *The Economist*, July 17, 2008.

[21] *The Lexus and the Olive Tree*, Thomas L. Friedman, Farrar Straus Giroux, 1999, page 172

[22] *Innovation Nation*, John Kao, Free Press, 2007, pages 188-189

[23] *Management: Tasks, Responsibilities, Practices* by Peter F. Drucker, Harper & Row, 1973

[24] *Innovation Nation*, John Kao, Free Press, 2007, page 188-189

[25] "The Fading Lustre of Clusters," *The Economist*, October 11, 2007.

[26] "Innovation: A Dark Art No More," *The Economist*, October 11, 2007.

[27] *High-Growth SMEs and Employment*, OECD, 2002.

[28] *The Job Generation Process* by David L Birch, Massachusetts Institute of Technology, Program on Neighborhood and Regional Change., 1979.

[29] "The Tortoise and the Hare," *The Economist*, January 19, 2006.

[30] *Innovation Nation*, John Kao, Free Press, 2007, pages 59-60.

[31] *Doing Business 2009: Comparing Regulation in 181 Countries*, The World Bank (www.doingbusiness.org)

[32] *Strategic Intuition* by William Duggan, Columbia Business School Publishing, 2007

[33] *Innovation Nation*, John Kao, Free Press, 2007, page 71.

[34] *Where Do Innovations Come From? Transformations in the US National Innovation System, 1970-2006*, by Fred Block and Matthew R. Keller, The Information Technology and Innovation Foundation, July 2008.

[35] "Innovation: A Dark Art No More," *The Economist*, October 11, 2007.

[36] "Is Internet Addiction Real" by Tori deAngelis, *Monitor on Psychology*, Volume 31, No. 4, April 2000.

[37] "Internet Use is Causing Social Isolation in the US, Study Finds" by John Markoff, *The New York Times*, February 17, 2000; "Study Links Internet, Social Contact" by Killeen Hanson, *The Stanford Daily*, February 28, 2005.

[38] "Teenagers at Risk of Internet Addiction" by Louise Williams and Tim Colquhoun, The Age (www.theage.com/au/technology), November 23, 2005.

[39] Center for Internet Addiction Recovery, www.netaddiction.com

[40] "WTF!? Internet Addiction Nominated for Entry in the Manual of Mental Disorders" by Katharine Gammon, *WIRED*, May 19, 2008.

[41] www.usdoj.gov/criminal/cybercrime/cyberstalking.htm

[42] "Sex and the Internet: Challenging the Myths" by Nancy Willard, Education World, www.education-world.com.

[43] "Networking Community: The Internet in Everyday Life" by Barry Wellman, Jeffrey Boase, Wenhong Chen, Keith Hampton, Anabel Quan-Haase, and Isabel Diaz de Isla, NetLab, the Center for Urban and Community Studies, University of Toronto.

[44] Ibid.

[45] "Social Impact of Broadband Internet: A Case Study in the Shippahagan Area, A Rural Zone in Atlantic Canada" by Sid-Ahmed Selouani, University of Moncton at Shippahagan, and Habib Hamam, University of Moncton at Moncton.

[46] "Online Communities: Networks that Nurture Long-Distance Relationships and Local Ties" by John B. Horrigan, Senior Researchter, Pew Internet & American Life Project, October 31, 2001.

[47] *Grown Up Digital: How the Net Generation is Changing Your World*, Don Tapscott, McGraw-Hill, 2008.

[48] *Living and Learning With New Media: Summary of Findings from the Digital Youth Project* by Mizuko Ito, Heather Horst, Matteo Bittanti, Danah Boyd, Becky Herr-Stephenson, Patricia Lange, C.J. Pascoe and Laura Robinson, The John D. and Catherine T. MacArthur Foundation, November 2008.

[49] Facebook user statistics from the company Web site (www.facebook.com/press/info.php?statistics); LinkedIn statistics from company press release, " LinkedIn Raises $22.7 Million from Goldman Sachs, The McGraw-Hill Companies, SAP Ventures and Bessemer Venture Partners" issued October 23, 2008.

[50] "End of Speculation: The Real Twitter Usage Numbers" by Michael Arrington, TechCrunch (www.techcrunch.com), April 29, 2008.

[51] "Internet, Social Capital and Democracy in the Information Age: Korea's Defeat Movement, the Red Devils, Candle Light Anti-US Demonstration, and Presidential Election During 2000-2002" by Jongwoo Han, Assistant Professor, Department of Political Science, Maxwell School of Citizenship and Public Affairs, Syracuse University, September 2002.